At-Risk Students

Transforming Student Behavior

Charisse Beach

ROWMAN & LITTLEFIELD EDUCATION
A division of
ROWMAN & LITTLEFIELD
Lanham • Boulder • New York • Toronto • Plymouth, UK

Published by Rowman & Littlefield Education
A division of Rowman & Littlefield
4501 Forbes Boulevard, Suite 200, Lanham, Maryland 20706
www.rowman.com

10 Thornbury Road, Plymouth PL6 7PP, United Kingdom

British Library Cataloguing in Publication Information Available

Library of Congress Cataloging-in-Publication Data is available

ISBN 978-1-4758-0706-6 (cloth : alk. paper)
ISBN 978-1-4758-0707-3 (pbk. : alk. paper)
ISBN 978-1-4758-0708-0 (electronic)

♾️™ The paper used in this publication meets the minimum requirements of American
National Standard for Information Sciences Permanence of Paper for Printed Library
Materials, ANSI/NISO Z39.48-1992.

Printed in the United States of America

This book is dedicated to my grandson, Elijah Armani Beach.

You are the destination that validates my journey.

Contents

Foreword

The dilemma faced by at-risk students is not a school or school district problem; it is a nation's problem; an American problem; even a global problem. Whether presented by the United States Department of Education, educational researchers, or school districts and schools across the country, the facts about the school engagement and academic achievement of at-risk students are disturbing. On all of the indicators of academic achievement, educational attainment, and school success, at-risk students are noticeably distinguished from other segments of the American population by their consistent clustering at the bottom. With few exceptions, these dismal patterns exist in urban, suburban, and rural school districts throughout the United States. Nationally, one sub-group (African-American males), are more likely than any other group to be suspended and expelled from school (Fergus 2009). In most American cities, dropout rates for African-American males are well above 50 percent, and they're less likely to enroll or graduate from college than any other group.

These patterns have become so common and widespread that a recitation of the numbers no longer generates alarm or even surprise. The real danger is that too many educators and too many members of our society have begun to accept this dismal state of affairs as the norm. The most important underlying challenge is to undermine that acceptance and create a new norm in which the facts are no longer acceptable or worse yet, expected as a matter of course.

At- Risk Students: Transforming Student Behavior is a refreshing look at what's working in America's schools. Moreover, it is a great example of what can happen when committed adults in schools and communities "create conditions for teaching and learning" (Peters, 2011). Charisse Beach does a great job of offering the reader three levels of educational thought: Perspective, Implications, and a way forward. At times, public education gets stopped in its tracks gaining the right perspective. The work of Beach presents the perspective and goes a step further to introduce the implications associated with it, but provides specific strategies and solutions as a way forward for our students at-risk to gain and sustain viable solutions to what life and schools have generally offered them in the past.

It will take political and personal will and the best efforts of all of us to overcome the challenges posed by this truly human dilemma. Biases, fears, and deeply held assumptions about At-risk students work against their school success. The biggest obstacle to students' success is the adults who believe they cannot succeed and the behaviors follow from that belief (Boykin and Noguera, 2010).

At- Risk Students: Transforming Student Behavior gives us hope and a way to shift paradigms from problems to solutions. As I work with school leaders and teachers around the country, they share their desire for practical strategies that they can implement immediately in their schools and class-rooms. I am indeed honored to introduce them to this book and the contents contained within. It will make a difference in the lives' of our children and those who capture, inspire, and teach them daily!

Stephen G. Peters,
Author, CEO and President of "The Peters Group"
June 2013

Preface

As I open my eyes and begin to focus on my surroundings, the bright lights overhead invade the remaining haze in my mind. As I lay here, I realize that tubes are coming out of parts of my body that I can no longer feel. I wonder, *"What stage of life am I in? Am I alive or have I transitioned to the other side?"* I can't feel anything. I'm just lying here, motionless.

Suddenly I hear voices and realize I'm not alone; there are others in the room with me. My oldest son, Robert, and several of my nearest and dearest family and friends are in the room with me as well. One by one, my loved ones surround the hospital bed and look down on me. Some of them offer words of encouragement, while others look at me then turn away to cry as if I can't see their despair. I sense fear and sadness all around me. I feel like I'm on display at a museum.

Inside I'm screaming all the encouragement *they* need to hear—*I* need to hear, but nothing comes out. I want to shout at them and tell them that I will live! I *have* to live! But I can't speak. My eyes search the faces gathered around the bed and then it hits me; someone is missing—Oliver. I close my eyes to fight back the tears when I realize my youngest son is the reason I'm here.

The impetus for this book stems from my personal journey with Oliver. I have the unique circumstance of being both an educator and the parent of an at-risk student, my son Oliver. I wrote *At-Risk Students: Transforming Student Behavior* as a result of the frustration I experienced as parent and educator while Oliver progressed through the education system. Unfortunately, Oliver's at-risk behaviors landed me in the hospital near death and landed him in an Illinois state penitentiary.

It was not until Oliver entered high school that I quickly learned that conventional consequences often fail to correct or eliminate undesirable behaviors in at-risk youth. Little did I know that my battles with the education system and with my own son would prepare me for writing a book with the purpose to provide educators with researched and proven strategies that have helped me to educate at-risk students.

The research for this work is based on my experiences as a mother/ educator as well as countless hours analyzing statistics from the National At-Risk Education Network, The Children's Defense Fund, and researching the works of experts in the field of at-risk youth such as Joyce Taylor-Gibson, *Educating the Throw-Away Children: What We Can Do to Help Students at Risk* and H. Richard Milner's *Start Where You Are, But Don't Stay There: Understanding Diversity, Opportunity Gaps, and Teaching in Today's Classrooms*.

My journey while writing this book has been very cathartic. I was compelled to write a book that offered alternative strategies that successfully dealt with the cause and effect of the at-risk behaviors our youth exhibit. My hope is that the strategies I've developed will help to fill the gap that currently exists within the education system by helping other educators to transform the lives of at-risk students using my methods.

Acknowledgments

I am grateful for the opportunity to motivate school leaders to examine a behavior-management system designed to educate and transform the lives of at-risk students.

To my son, Robert, I know you have suffered as your idyllic little family morphed into an altered universe; yet, you proudly took your rightful place as our family's patriarch. You are loved. To my wonderful daughter-in-law Nicole, thank you for bringing balance and joy to our family. To my niece, Jasmine, you demonstrate that adversities can be conquered and youth at risk can become successful. I am very proud of you! To my best friend of over thirty years, Cheryl Pickenpack Wilson, thank you for that fateful phone call on August 20, 2007. Elliot Weinshenker, for remaining steadfast in your unwavering support and generosity to my family and me, I sincerely thank you.

Thank you, Jeff May, for providing me with the opportunity to serve at-risk students. To my Premier Academy-Joliet staff, thank you for having done the hard work that makes this book relevant. Thank you, Kim Gordon, for your convictions on instructional best practices that support that all students can learn when educators teach well. To my peer review team: Minnie Doss, Mary Griffin, and Victoria Jones, I appreciate your commitment to excellence and the many, many hours you sacrificed.

Finally, thank you, Abby Herman, for the best editing expertise and timely turnaround imaginable, and to Rowman & Littlefield Education for publishing my book.

In loving memory of my mother and father, Ollie M. Smothers and Robert L. Coleman, and my dear friend, Dorothy Marie Carroll; you are my angels.

And to my son, Oliver, I love you always and this too shall pass . . .

Introduction

A wise man was taking a sunrise walk along a beach. He came upon a young man who was picking up starfish from the sand and tossing them gently back into the ocean.
"What are you doing?" the wise man asked.
"The sun is coming up and the tide is going out. If I don't throw them back, they will die," was the young man's response.

Figure 0.1.

To that, the wise man replied, "But there are miles and miles of beach and millions of starfish. You cannot possibly make a difference."
The young man bent down, picked up another starfish, and threw it lovingly back beyond the breaking waves. "I made a difference for that one," he replied.

Loren Eiseley, *The Star Thrower* (1969)

Students are considered at risk when they experience a significant mismatch between their circumstances and needs, and the capacity or willingness of the school to accept, accommodate, and respond to them in a manner that supports and enables their social, emotional, and intellectual growth and development. Many students fit this definition and most of these students are not given the support they need to grow beyond their current circumstance, not for lack of effort on the part of the school, but for lack of knowledge of how best to serve these youth.

Researchers such as Mark Lipsey and James Derzon believe the root causes of at-risk behavior and violence begin in the elementary grades with attention deficits, hyperactivity or learning disorders, early aggressive behavior, low IQ, poor behavioral control, low self-esteem, and family conflict. Studies also show that it is crucial that at-risk behaviors be identified early and reevaluated regularly to prevent undesirable behavior and unprovoked outbursts of violence. Traditional school systems rarely provide adequate or appropriate support for at-risk students.

The expectation of student violence creates a moral panic among educators. We make assumptions about a student's home life that often taints our professional responsibilities and encourages us to justify why these students won't be successful. However, when we delve deeper into how these characteristics severely compromise student success, we begin to unravel the myths that surround at-risk behaviors and begin to rebuild on a foundation of action and support to help us adequately deal with at-risk behaviors in today's youth.

School violence is the umbrella covering all at-risk behaviors. It can adversely traumatize the victim(s), perpetrator(s), the school, and the community at large. Today, there are various myths that exist about at-risk behaviors and violence in schools.

MYTH: School violence happens among children from problem homes or uneducated families.

FACT: School violence affects children across all racial, social, economic, and geographical boundaries. No child is immune from school violence just because they attend school in a good school district, attend an expensive prep school, or study abroad. There are many instances where violence in school erupts among children from stellar homes with parents who are highly educated and have provided their children with the best of everything. Consider the two most horrific incidents of school violence on record to date: Columbine High School and Sandy Hook Elementary; both incidents were perpetrated by youth who attended schools in stellar school districts and had parents of substantial financial means.

MYTH: If you don't want trouble, you should just look the other way.

FACT: Turning away and pretending that you haven't seen violence in school only increases the possibility that not only will it happen again, but the next time the violence may escalate and more children may be hurt or even killed.

MYTH: If you ignore violence in school it will go away in time.

FACT: Many children who commit violent acts do so because they think they can get away with it. If there is no fear of getting caught or being punished, the violence continues to escalate and often provides the offender with an adrenaline rush and a false sense of power.

MYTH: Children who commit violent acts in school should be locked away until they learn how to live productively within society.

FACT: Committing children to permanent incarceration for violent acts is often an indication that the education system and society have failed them in some way. There are numerous reasons why children who exhibit at-risk behaviors find themselves incarcerated. Deteriorating family structure, mental health challenges, poverty, addictions, gang violence, teen pregnancy, and truancy have all been identified as characteristics that put youth at risk.

According to the National Center for Injury Prevention and Control, Division of Violence Prevention, a number of factors can increase the risk of youth engaging in violence at school; things such as alcohol and drug use, depression, anxiety, and many other psychological problems result in at-risk behavior. Finding the cause of their behavior and treating the cause to effect a cure is a logical solution to combating the violence.

MYTH: There is no solution to school violence.

FACT: Educating parents, teachers, students, and the community on how to identify at-risk behaviors in an attempt to prevent senseless violence is why *At-Risk Students: Transforming Student Behavior* was written.

At-Risk Students was written for district administrators, school administrators and department heads, teachers, individuals employed in a traditional public or charter school system in grades 6–12, anyone employed in an alternative school working with at-risk students, as well as anyone looking to incorporate a comprehensive behavior system into their strategic school-improvement plans as a response to intervention. This book is a must-read supplement for graduate students seeking a degree in educational administration.

At-Risk Students was designed as a resource for educators to explore a succinct, comprehensive behavior system.

Educators will be provided with the tools to: expeditiously identify at-risk characteristics; incorporate policies that support and monitor their achievement; implement research-based strategies designed to create a positive school culture that promotes teaching and learning.

Expeditiously identify at-risk characteristics.

Poverty, violence, addiction, homelessness, and undiagnosed/untreated mental illness are serious problems that many students face in today's world, which can seriously affect academic success and school safety. Often times, both students and parents are at risk and in need of support services in order to become stable. It is critical that these characteristics are identified quickly, so that the appropriate intervention can be implemented.

Incorporate policies that support and monitor their achievement.

Successfully educating at-risk students is costly. Therefore, policies must be developed and implemented on a number of levels. At-risk students must be challenged to develop academic and nonacademic skills and competencies. Administrators, teachers, and support staff must engage in behaviors that facilitate persistence and completion of the interventions. At the community level, businesses and community-based organizations must form partnerships with schools and school districts in order to increase the opportunities for students and families at risk.

Implement research-based strategies designed to create a positive school culture that promotes teaching and learning.

To achieve success among at-risk students by the twenty-first century, a variety of strategies must be implemented. In addition to these strategies, academic support services must be offered that include developing and building skills for at-risk students and the teachers who work with them. Furthermore, the provision of social support is vital. It can come from counselors, faculty, parents, family, and other students. This framework brings together the student, the teacher, the school, parents, and the community in a dynamic synthesis.

Schools or programs working with at-risk youth should specifically address the at-risk behaviors exhibited by them in both the home and in school. To achieve an effective intervention, the school, home, and the community must work together and invest in helping them to overcome their obstacles. In the end, educators will have the tools necessary to organize the educational structure of their school or district around a comprehensive behavior system that will educate and transform the lives of at-risk students.

Chapter One

Achievement Disparities

According to ethnic and racial disparities in education, African American, American Indian, Latino, and Southeast Asian groups underperform academically relative to Caucasians and other Asian Americans. More often than not, these educational disparities are reflected in test scores used to assess academic achievement, percentages of students repeating one or more grades, dropout and decreasing graduation rates, and suspension and expulsion rates. This is why understanding the methods used to engage students during the learning process is critical to academic achievement across ethnic and racial groups.

All too often, test scores and other standardized procedures are used to track students' ability, skill level, and knowledge of educational material. The overreliance on tests scores, both school and individual, has the effect of stigmatizing students who do not test well and reinforces stereotypes that might be addressed if educators focused more on teaching and learning rather than learning outcomes derived from test scores.

Too much testing and not enough teaching will not eliminate the achievement gap. School systems that purport to take into account the diversity of their students in terms of standardized tests, educational materials, pedagogy, and content are "antithetical to diversity because it suggests that all students live and operate in homogeneous environments with equality of opportunity afforded to them," according to H. Richard Milner IV, an associate professor of education at Vanderbilt University, in his book *Start Where You Are, But Don't Stay There: Understanding Diversity, Opportunity Gaps, and Teaching in Today's Classrooms*. It is often the case, however, that students are placed in tracking groups (based on testing) as a means of tailoring lesson plans for different types of learners.

However, many minority students are vastly overrepresented in lower educational track programs. In addition, minority students are often inadvertently placed into lower track programs because teachers and administrators have lower expectations for minority students. Such low expectations can be viewed as a form of institutional racism and racial segregation. And once minority students are placed in lower track programs or schools, they tend to have less-qualified teachers, less-challenging curriculum, and fewer opportunities to advance into higher track programs.

Whether the difference is between socioeconomic or ethnic groups across geographic locations, inequality persists. On one hand, some researchers claim that educational inequality is due to social class and family background; while others argue that inadequately managed schools bear most of the responsibility for low student achievement. In contrast, many educators believe that achievement disparities are the result of inappropriate student behavior being inconsistently and improperly addressed.

Many teachers argue that among African American students, achievement disparities exist primarily because of students' lack of motivation to learn, failure to attend classes, lack of preparation for school, inability to focus in class, participation in street culture, or failure to behave appropriately in class. Further hindering their success are parents who cultivate inappropriate values that are inconsistent with those of the school.

Such beliefs directly correlate with teachers disconnecting or disengaging parents with regard to student behaviors. Or they assume parents do not have the time, interest, money, or energy to support what their children are doing while at school. This assumption, in conjunction with the inappropriate behavior, is seen as justification for students' underachievement. Consequently, students end up being blamed for their own circumstances, lose confidence in the adults around them, and begin to depend solely on each other. As a result, they push further away from school, which results in them being designated at risk.

There is much concern about the achievement gap that exists among African American students (particularly African American males) in terms of their successful completion of high school. However, due to a variety of reasons, many African American students do not meet the traditional criteria for achievement and cannot or will not conform to the parochial values in traditional school systems.

In light of this fact, achievement disparities among African American students will only decrease when educators shift from their stereotypical bias and prejudice beliefs and attitudes that caused the gap in the first place—it starts with educators raising their awareness about what it means to be an at-risk youth. When educators become aware of students' attitudes about their learning environment then, and only then, will lasting change take place.

The Children's Defense Fund (CDF) reports that although no students are immune from suspension, African American students are suspended at twice the rate of any other ethnic group. The CDF report states that although African American children account for 27.1 percent of school children, they represent 42.3 percent of suspended children. Furthermore, data collected shows 12.8 percent of African American students are suspended as compared with 4.1 percent of white students. In short, three times the amount of African American students is suspended from school on a regular basis versus their white counterparts.

Oftentimes, African American students are labeled as at risk because of their continued disengagement from school, poor academic performance, high rates of absenteeism, suspension, expulsion, or dropout rates. Among these are a rising number of African American males who question the status quo when they find themselves in a school setting where the values of white, middle-class society dominate.

For their part, these young men either conform to or resist the under-achiever stereotype. The conformist student internalizes the underachiever mentality and believes that academic work is not for him. Or the student resists, and therefore views conforming as simply a coping mechanism, because doing otherwise would be to go against a system that he believes has failed him. This mindset has created a new class of at-risk student—the student who is so alienated by the hostility of the school environment that he or she leaves the environment.

Obviously, teachers play a pivotal role in the construction of students as underachievers and their designation of students as at risk. Several studies have examined teachers' beliefs about low-performing African American males in high school and found a substantial majority of the teachers attributed students' academic failures to the students, their parents, and their community, rather than to their teaching. Arguably, based on statistics, teaching African American males can be very challenging; however, the most significant way to help close the achievement gap is for educators to build relationships of mutual trust and respect with students.

One way teachers can establish mutual trust and respect between student and teacher—particularly at-risk students—is to incorporate the students' background into instruction. Teachers should welcome students every day with a sincere greeting. Something as simple as a warm smile and saying "good morning" lets students know you care. Once students realize that the teacher cares about them, it's easy to have open dialogue. It's during that dialogue that teachers will learn something about the students and what matters most in their world. Students reject superficial attachments and may shut down and stop communicating if they sense insincerity.

PATH of AT-RISK STUDENTS:

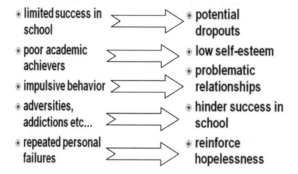

- Disproportionate number of males and minorities are labeled at-risk.

- Many at-risk students come from homes where school policies are not understood and/ or unappreciated.

- Research indicates students from such environments will frequently create situations that place home and school at odds with each other.

- This home-school disconnection is the formula for failure that encourages students to seek alternate lifestyle choices.

- Many at-risk students attend large or departmentalized schools, where they receive daily instruction from several different teachers.

- Research indicates students in such schools tend to feel more alienated from their teachers and peers.

- The feeling of alienation often leads to discipline problems.

Figure 1.1.

At-risk students thrive better when they can make an immediate, real-world connection, as they are often limited in their long-range thinking. One way teachers can learn more about their students is to engage them in classroom discussion about current events. When teachers learn how their students feel about current events, the foundation is laid for making a deeper, more personal connection. Teachers should strive to drill down the engagement from large group, to small group, to individual engagements as a best practice to create open dialogue with their students.

As the relationship grows, teachers learn about their students' goals and dreams and what matters to them. It's beneficial for teachers to help students streamline their focus in order to help students reach their goals and realize their dreams by creating an active learning environment. In order to accomplish this, teachers must provide students with criteria rather than rules and model the behaviors they wish to see exhibited in their students. Children model what they see over what they hear!

At-risk students are usually apathetic toward everything, which is why they struggle to be successful in and outside of school. They tend to have minimal identification with school. They may have disciplinary or truancy problems, which often leads to credit deficiency; or they may exhibit impulsive behavior, which usually leads to problematic peer relationships. Fortunately, there is hope. Most students will work for something they want as opposed to avoiding a punishment or consequence. The key is to encourage students to strive to do their best and go above and beyond what they normally would do.

By default, the school system has become the primary battleground to address youth who exhibit at-risk behaviors. School districts readily admit that they are inadequately prepared for this immense task, yet this fact has not stopped educators from taking on the noble effort to address the problem. Public education has taken a much-needed shift from recycling initiatives to creating initiatives that increase achievement in today's at-risk learners.

School districts across the nation are establishing Professional Learning Communities (PLCs), designed to create best practices. Defined in *Revisiting Professional Learning Communities at Work: New Insights for Improving Schools* by Richard DuFour, Rebecca DuFour, and Robert Eaker, education authorities at Solution Tree, a PLC is "an ongoing process in which educators work collaboratively in recurring cycles of collective inquiry and action research to achieve better results for the students they serve" (p. 14).Schools must become a model for equal opportunity and a place where the student's need for achievement and positive experiences can be met.

ESSENTIAL IDEAS TO REMEMBER

In today's public schools, success for African Americans is too often elusive. Our society still bears the legacy of exclusion and low expectations for African American children, and our public-education system has not adequately responded to remedy this situation. This persistent challenge is deeply harmful to the African American students. African American males are more likely than any other group to be suspended from school. They are underrepresented in programs for the highly capable, overrepresented in special-education programs, and outperformed consistently by African American females.

Lower rates of high-school graduation lead to less employment, higher rates of incarceration, ill health, substance abuse, and intergenerational poverty. But while we cannot change the past, we can and must change the education system that shapes our future. An education system that welcomes, respects, and engages African American students is achievable. Closing the education gap is achievable.

In order for this achievement to take place, students need good teachers as role models. Diverse, culturally knowledgeable, experienced, and highly qualified teachers can help narrow the achievement gap and serve as models for children who will live in multicultural environments. Children of color also need teachers who look like them, who share similar cultural experiences, and who can be role models to demonstrate the efficacy of education and achievement.

Poor and minority students often get less-qualified teachers. Low-performing schools are frequently unable to attract and retain effective and experienced teachers. Unfortunately, low-performing schools also tend to serve large numbers of poor and minority students. In an attempt to resolve this situation, the teacher equity clause in the federal No Child Left Behind Act mandates that states ensure that teachers of core subjects are "highly qualified" and that poor and minority children are not taught at higher rates than other children by inexperienced and/or unqualified teachers.

Teachers must be adept at meeting specific needs of students, and be careful not to misidentify an anger or behavioral problem as a learning disability. Good teachers will take extra steps to relate to all of their students; "high-quality" teachers have a passion for teaching each student, and take the time to learn the background of their students so they can help overcome challenges those students bring to school.

Closing the achievement gap will require commitment to aligning efforts across the education system. State, school district, and school building leadership can help perpetuate the achievement gap, or it can be a powerful force for eliminating it. When school boards, superintendents, and principals make closing the gap a top priority—and when they plan, allocate resources, and design accountability measures to do so—they make progress.

Perhaps most important, education leaders who have made progress in narrowing the achievement gap are those who have a sense of urgency and a deep moral conviction that this work is central to their purpose as educators. These are the educators who have the courage to challenge the status quo, to build the political will for change, and to inspire their communities to sustain the work of making schools work for everyone.

The disparity between various demographic groups of students is commonly referred to as the "achievement gap." In actuality, a number of different gaps exist that result in this phenomenon of low achievement. These include an opportunity gap, resource gap, readiness-to-learn gap, and a preparation gap of teachers, constituting an overall education gap. The unequal education of African American students is evidenced by:

- System-wide low expectations
- Ongoing and widening achievement gaps
- Underinvolvement in school activities other than sports
- Overrepresentation in special education programs
- Disproportionate discipline referrals, resulting in suspension and expulsion
- Overrepresentation in the juvenile justice system
- Less access and effective use of technology

Chapter Two

Parents At Risk

Parents of at-risk children may experience feelings of inadequacy and create chaos with authority figures at school. For example, a parent who becomes homeless may challenge a principal's decision of suspension because his or her child will lose the six hours of guaranteed shelter and the one to two meals the child would receive if he or she were in school. At that point, explaining the discipline policy and school rules will offer little comfort to the desperate parent. The best strategy is to provide the parent with local resources and be compassionate but firm.

The students who require the most redirection often have parents who demand the most time, worry, and energy from school leaders. It is important to think positively about at-risk students, and it is equally important to keep that focus when dealing with their parents. There are few absolutes in education. Every rule has an exception and no matter how consistent educators attempt to be, there are times when plans must be adjusted.

However, one rule that should never be broken is educators must refrain from arguing, yelling, using sarcasm, or behaving unprofessionally. There are several reasons to adopt this practice. One of them is that in every situation there needs to be at least one adult, and the only person you can rely on to act as the adult is you. It isn't a good idea to argue with difficult people because you will not win, at least not during the argument. Difficult people may find themselves in constant conflict. They argue at home, are confrontational at work, exhibit road rage, and display agitation with neighbors.

When parents are angry, getting them calm so they can hear what is being said is an important step toward addressing their concerns. Clearly state, "Please don't talk to me like that. I will never speak to you like that, and I will never speak to your child like that. And no one in this school will ever speak to you or your child like that." If this is a phone call, you may inform the parent that you are hanging up the phone now and look forward to speaking with him or her after he or she has calmed down. In a face-to-face meeting, politely excuse yourself, inviting the parents back when they are composed.

One of the best diffusers in a heated situation is to apologize. However, the specific wording is important because it can help us calm the waters and yet retain our dignity. It is very difficult to say, "I was wrong." It is even more difficult to say it when it is not true. But there is one way we can approach all situations that will help satisfy even the most hostile parents while allowing us to be honest, and that is to say, "I am sorry for what happened."

Five powerful words to use when communicating with difficult parents are, "Thank you for your support." Even if the parent has no intention of offering support, when you say it, the degree of strife diminishes. Also, imagine calling a parent to inform them that their child has earned a Saturday school detention. Notice I say "earned" instead of "got." People *earn* awards but *get* traffic tickets.

The impetus for developing positive parent communication when working with our most challenging parents is very simple: It will make our lives easier. Administrators must work with parents who are angry with them or their schools. If a parent's concern isn't successfully resolved, the problem—and the parent's feelings—will continue to fester and will likely escalate.

A second and equally important reason for administrators to develop successful techniques is to teach the teachers. This is something that must be done in order to help teachers confidently, effectively, and productively interact with parents. School leaders can teach others—students, parents, and staff members—new ways to interact. We have a responsibility to consistently model appropriate behavior to everyone with whom we come in contact.

Simply exhorting teachers to contact parents more often will not change anything. If we would like our new teachers, as well as our more experienced staff members, to initiate contact with parents, it is important that they learn how. It is unrealistic to expect all faculty members to inherently know how to talk to parents. Administrators have numerous opportunities to refine and enhance our communication skills with parents. However, even our most veteran faculty members may not have received or made as many phone calls in their entire career as administrators do in one semester.

For teachers to initiate more contact with parents and be more comfortable with them, we must teach teachers what to say. Developing a particular approach to doing something that they are unfamiliar or uncomfortable with can be very helpful in building up their confidence. Perhaps encouraging teachers to write down what they want to say and even a couple of topics to bring up in case the conversation fizzles can be helpful and a confidence-builder.

Not only is dealing with angry or unreasonable parents upsetting, it's time-consuming. It's only natural for parents to want the best for their child. Every now and then there are parents who refuse to accept that their child struggles in school. It can be easy for them to make excuses and blame others for their child's troubles. Before you know it, you have a huge problem on your hands. Here are some strategies to help you resolve difficult situations with parents.

1. Let upset parents know that your goal is to help every child succeed. Look for ways to find common ground. Tell parents that both of you want what's best for their child and that you want to find ways to work together. When parents are able to look at the big picture and realize that you are on the same side, you can begin to work together to help their child succeed.

2. No matter how tense a situation becomes, always remember that your student is someone's precious baby. Open your conversation with parents by acknowledging the child's strengths before you focus on areas of concern.

3. Good records that document dates, times, notes, and decisions about students can be invaluable if problems arise. Electronic parent contact logs come in handy if you ever need to document how you've involved and informed parents after an incident at school. After making phone calls to parents to discuss problems, take a few minutes to record any important information that was discussed. Make sure to date notes that you receive from parents before you file them in the folders. If you respond to a parent's note in writing, make a copy of your response and staple it to the parent's note.

4. Be prepared to give specific examples to illustrate the points you make. Show parents examples of average and above average work for your grade level. White out the names on papers and use actual samples of students' work to clearly illustrate typical work for the grade level. The idea isn't to compare students to one another; it's to give parents a clear idea of exactly what your expectations are for students in your class.

5. Have you ever been caught off guard by a parent and answered a question in a way that you regret later? If a parent asks you a question that floors you, don't be put on the spot. It's fine to let parents know that you need some time to reflect on their question before you respond. Let them know that you'll get back to them in a day or two. Relax—you've just bought yourself time to explore options and perhaps bounce ideas off of a colleague before you respond to the parents.

6. Again, don't be afraid to end a meeting with parents who become confrontational. Sometimes, the best thing to do is to provide an op-

portunity for all parties to cool down and reflect on the issues at hand by bringing the meeting to a close. Set a time and date to meet again. If you feel threatened, ask for district-level support to attend the next conference.

7. It can be awkward when parents share too much information with you. While it's helpful to know things that directly impact a student, it can be problematic when parents disclose too much personal information. It's not your job to be their therapist. Remind parents that during the limited time you have to speak with them, that you need to focus on their child and not on them.

8. Sometimes neighborhood issues spill over into the classroom. Don't let yourself get dragged into disputes between families of children in your school. Problems escalate quickly if it's perceived that you're siding with other parents. When parents begin to share information about neighborhood squabbles, jump right in and tell them that it's information that you don't need to hear. Let parents know that you're receptive to their thoughts and ideas about their child, but you must stay out of personal issues between the families.

ESSENTIAL IDEAS TO REMEMBER

Parents are children's first teachers and many do not understand how early learning influences a child's future success in school. Parents at risk need extra guidance on the importance of reading to their children, choosing child-care providers who will help prepare their children for school, and understanding what "parental involvement" really entails in building children's social and academic skills. They need to know what kind of resources are out there to support them, and how to begin to navigate the school system before their children enter it.

Parents of at-risk children need strong support from teachers and other staff, and they must feel welcome when they walk in the school doors. Active parents help improve teaching. Parents at risk often threaten the moral fiber of the school and schools are not always welcoming to those parents. Genuine invitations to visit the school are important and help parents in need to become strong teaching partners.

Many parents are focused on survival, or have had bad experiences in school. They need help understanding the importance of an education, and sharing that value with their children. Parents are clearly seen as critical role models in motivating their children to succeed, but parents at risk need support. Many are ill-equipped to help their children navigate school and homework, and cultural and language barriers pose further problems. They need help understanding the resources available to support them and their children. Along with the resources, value and acceptance from their child's school will matter most in the long term.

Chapter Three

Characteristics of At-Risk Students

Do you think you would know if a child or teen was up to something illegal or dangerous? Do you believe that you would know if he or she was involved in gang activity? Would you know if a child was a bully? Would your own son or daughter come to you if they were being bullied or beaten up at school? Oftentimes the parents of the victims as well as the teachers of the kids responsible for school violence have no idea that anything is going on.

Even the best parents and teachers can sometimes fail to realize that a child is having a problem at school or is headed down a dangerous path. Teens especially can be evasive and hard to read and many indiscretions tend to get chalked up to typical teen angst and growing pains. This chapter will help schools to differentiate between growing pains and a serious problem and help you to recognize the sign of trouble before it's too late. In addition to educating our youth, schools are now responsible for keeping children safe so they can focus on their education, rather than worrying about their safety.

According to the Education Resource Information Center, the following characteristics serve as indicators of at-risk student behaviors. Arguably, there are other characteristics not discussed in this chapter that are equally disruptive; but the ones explored here tend to prevail more often without adequate interventions. Often, these characteristics mask themselves as factors of a student's environment and are, therefore, unmovable. To the contrary, each characteristic should be consistently addressed with urgency.

The topics covered in this section are geared to help schools and teachers to identify students who may be in trouble or at risk of being a victim or instigator of school violence or crime of any kind. Knowing the signs could mean life or death in some cases, so please take some time to read through the information here and discuss it with your students or own children whether you believe there is a problem or not.

	Characteristic	No	Yes	Not Sure
1	Multiple suspensions, expelled, and/or truant			
2	Verbally abusive			
3	Struggles with basic family rules and expectations			
4	Refuses to do basic household chores/homework			
5	Problems with the law/authority			
6	Parents have to pick words carefully to avoid a verbal attack/rage			
7	In danger of dropping out of high school			
8	Associates with a suspect peer group			
9	Lost interest in activities, sports, hobbies, and/or childhood friends			
10	Evidence of suicide			
11	Depressed /withdrawn			
12	Violent behavior			
13	Sexually promiscuous			
14	Appearance or personal hygiene changes			
15	Deceitful and manipulative			
16	Caught stealing money or personal items from family and/or friends			
17	Sleeps excessively			
18	Displays outbursts of temper			
19	Lacks self-worth and self-esteem			
20	Defies established rules regardless of the consequences			
21	Parents feel powerless			
22	Suspects drugs or alcohol use			
23	Grades dropped			

Figure 3.1.

Every day in America . . .

- 208 children are arrested for violent crimes
- 487 children are arrested for drug abuse
- 1,825 children are confirmed abused or neglected
- 914 babies are born to teen mothers
- 2,712 babies are born into poverty
- 2857 children drop out of high school
- 4,500 children are arrested

EXPERIENCING LIMITED SUCCESS IN SCHOOL

Students experiencing limited success in school are often unable to choose the right subjects, attend classes regularly, listen and take good notes, study daily, and get involved in school activities. At-risk students vary enormously in talent. Some have very high ability, but show obvious signs of poor self-management, low motivation, or bad attitude. Others try hard, but are handicapped by below-average academic abilities. Both practices generally lead to credit deficiency.

At-risk students are often as ambitious as their counterparts (they also want to become doctors, lawyers, and business managers), but they possess misaligned ambitions. They find it difficult to fulfill their dreams because they are unaware of the steps that will help them to achieve their ambitions, which are often dreamlike and not realistically connected to specific educational and career paths. Regardless of how hard they try, they find themselves running in place, unsure of why they are in their current location or how they got there and even more unsure of how to reach their final destination.

LOW ACADEMIC ACHIEVERS

Typically, at-risk students earn lower-than-average grades. They have a vague idea of what is going on, but clearly have not mastered the material in their classes. The least-successful students appear to be the truly clueless, and rely on common sense rather than on resource material and lectures in a futile attempt to overcome their low level of preparation. Their work is often carelessly prepared, incomplete, inaccurate, inconsistent, late, or not submitted at all.

These students' obvious lack of preparation clearly communicates to teachers that their education is a low priority for them. Their idea of studying is to memorize terms and definitions in the hope that their teacher will ask them to merely regurgitate information on the test. When asked to comprehend, apply, analyze, synthesize, or evaluate information, they are often unable or unwilling to do so. Oftentimes, these students leave school and ultimately become another dropout statistic.

TRUANCY

Students who are regularly absent or tardy to class may be consumed with inappropriate relationships or conflicting obligations. It's appalling to hear a parent give the excuse that their student was absent because the parent had to work and didn't have a babysitter, or was late because they don't have an alarm clock. This teaches students that school attendance is not a priority. Other offenders may lack motivation, struggle with low self-esteem, or be plagued by addictions, abuse, or family adversities which prevent them from attending classes regularly or keeping up with the demands of their classes.

UNINTERESTED IN SCHOOL ACTIVITIES

Unproductive students are not committed to participating in school activities. In an effort to encourage at-risk students to become more involved and participate in enrichment activities, the federal government used its No Child Left Behind campaign to produce the twenty-first-Century Community Learning Centers (CCLC). The program's purpose was to provide opportunities for communities to establish or expand activities that focus on improved academic achievement, enrichment services that reinforce and complement the academic program, and family literacy and other related educational development services.

Impressed? Don't be. There is no relevant data to assess whether or not the program produced effective results. For the past ten years, CCLCs have served as a free babysitting service that often housed disruptive, uncommitted students. These students participate without enthusiasm, which frequently results in malignancy spreading to the other students. Instead, programs that empower youth to make positive lifestyle transformations provide a better foundation in overcoming academic and social pitfalls.

"Blueprints for Healthy Youth Development" is a research project within the Center for the Study and Prevention of Violence, at the University of Colorado Boulder. The Blueprints mission is to identify and disseminate evidence-based prevention and intervention programs that are effective in reducing antisocial behavior and promoting a healthy course of youth development. In doing so, Blueprints serves as a resource for governments, foundations, businesses, and other organizations trying to make informed judgments about their investments in youth programs.

One Blueprint program with proven results in decreasing at-risk student behaviors is Safe Harbor: A School Based Victim Assistance/Violence Prevention Program. The goals for the Safe Harbor program are to enhance student success and address self-esteem, anger management, conflict resolution, and social interaction in general and to develop strategies to deal with hatred, violence, and bullying in a positive and informative manner.

Another program with national recognition is Big Brothers Big Sisters of America (BBBSA). BBBSA began in the early twentieth century as a means to reach youth who were in need of socialization, firm guidance, and connection with positive adult role models. BBBSA, with a network of more than five hundred local programs throughout the nation, continues to operate as the largest and best-known mentoring organization in the United States, maintaining more than one hundred thousand one-to-one relationships between youth and volunteer adults. Volunteer mentors are screened and trained, and matches are made carefully using established procedures and criteria.

Individual BBBSA agencies adhere to national guidelines but customize their programs to fit local circumstances. The program serves youth ages six to eighteen, a significant number of whom are from disadvantaged single-parent households. A mentor meets with his or her mentee at least three times a month, participating in activities that enhance communication skills, develop relationship skills, and support positive decision making. Such activities are determined by the interests of the child and the volunteer and could include attending school activities or sporting events, visiting the library, or just sharing thoughts and ideas about life.

An eighteen-month study of eight BBBSA affiliates found that when compared with a control group on a waiting list for a match, youth in the mentoring program were 46 percent less likely to start using drugs, 27 percent less likely to start drinking, and 32 percent less likely to hit someone. Mentored youth skipped half as many days of school as control youth, had better attitudes toward and performance in school, and had improved peer and family relationships.

ADVERSITIES

Over the past twelve years as an administrator, I've held numerous parent conferences that began with parents confessing to negligence due to under-employment, health challenges, lack of resources, personal or family adversities, and so on. Parents or guardians are the first teachers in every child's life; what children learn from them is intrinsic in the child's academic and social-emotional development. Parenting practices in terms of inconsistent routines for children, limited monitoring of school performance, and failure to encourage high educational aspirations contribute to students' vulnerability to become at risk.

MENTAL HEALTH DISORDERS

Mental health disorders may interfere with a student's ability to function at school. If a student has a psychiatric disability, he or she may have trouble staying on task and following procedures as directed, and may experience difficulty screening out environmental stimuli such as sounds, sights, or smells; concentrating; handling multiple tasks; understanding and interpreting criticism; interacting with others; and responding to change such as unexpected glitches, new assignments, new assignment due dates, and different teachers. Placing students in special education is not the answer to all mental health issues.

Some students diagnosed with a mental health disorder such as attention deficit disorder or attention deficit hyperactivity disorder show limited to no signs of struggling in school. Others may require medication or specific accommodations to be carried out within the general education classroom. In this instance, parents should consider a 504 plan, part of the Rehabilitation Act of 1973 that prohibits discrimination based upon disability. Section 504 is an antidiscrimination, civil rights statute that requires the needs of students with disabilities to be met as adequately as the needs of the nondisabled are met.

IMPULSIVITY

Students who act impulsively do not consider the consequences of their behavior before they act. This directly affects how the student thinks, or, in some cases, doesn't think. It is often the case that in a perceived crisis, the student slips into survival mode, not at all open to reason or logic. As a result, impulsive behavior often results in various disciplinary interventions that ultimately fail. More importantly, students who exhibit risqué behaviors are more prone to be involved in acts of violence and/or court involvement.

COURT INVOLVEMENT

At-risk behaviors generally lead to court involvement. The juvenile justice system currently operates under the guise of a slap on the wrist or providing youth with a wake-up call to help them to alter their negative behaviors. Sometimes that works; most times it does not. A school–home–community model of education will better serve at-risk students who are being monitored by the court. This model is the fiber of providing wraparound support.

VICTIMIZATION

In many cases, at-risk students have been the victim of violence by adults, relatives, or other children in their lives. As a result, they bring special issues to school officials that require special care, protection, and compassion. Schools need to be especially sensitive to the signs of violence and abuse and be proactive in providing programs or services to students in need. Schools must be on the front line protecting the students they serve.

LOW SOCIOECONOMIC STATUS

Families from low-socioeconomic-status (SES) communities are less likely to have the financial resources to provide their children with academic support. Research indicates that children from low-SES households and communities develop academic skills more slowly compared to children from higher SES groups. Initial academic skills are correlated with the home environment, where low literacy environments and chronic stress negatively affect a child's preacademic skills.

The school systems in low-SES communities are often underresourced, negatively affecting students' academic progress. Inadequate education and increased dropout rates affect children's academic achievement, perpetuating the low-SES status of the community. Improving school systems and early-intervention programs may help to reduce these risk factors, and thus increased research on the correlation between SES and education is essential.

In 2007, approximately two hundred high-school students completed a checklist of traits that they recognized in themselves or their environment. Many at-risk students are burdened with daily living challenges, which make it clear that schools cannot effectively educate these children in the same way they educate their successful counterparts. At-risk students will not be passionate about learning. They will challenge authority. They will be unmotivated by rules, procedures, and consequences.

ESSENTIAL IDEAS TO REMEMBER

Nationally, over 25 percent of potential high-school graduates drop out before graduation. In some major cities the rate is 40 percent. Higher standards in the public schools have affected millions of minority and disadvantaged students who are "at risk." Educational reform has changed the rules before the system has had a chance to accommodate an increasing number of students who are dropping out and becoming a burden to society. The identification of at-risk students and the development of programs to prevent their failure are necessary components of educational reform.

What Are the Characteristics of At-Risk Students?

At-risk students are students who are not experiencing success in school and are potential dropouts. They are usually low academic achievers who exhibit low self-esteem. Disproportionate numbers of them are males and minorities. Generally they are from low-SES families. Students who are both low income and minority status are at higher risk; their parents may have low educational backgrounds and may not have high educational expectations for their children.

At-risk students tend not to participate in school activities and have a minimal identification with the school. They have disciplinary and truancy problems that lead to credit deficiency. They exhibit impulsive behavior and their peer relationships are problematic. Adversities, victimization, court involvement, and other problems prevent them from participating successfully in school. As they experience failure and fall behind their peers, school becomes a negative environment that reinforces their low self-esteem.

How Can At-Risk Students Be Identified?

At-risk students need to be identified as early as possible and regularly re-evaluated because their family status and living situations often change. Some researchers believe that the roots of at-risk behavior begin in the elementary grades with low achievement patterns, high absenteeism, and low self-esteem. Programs identifying and working with at-risk students are needed at every grade level.

Teachers should be well trained and alert to the symptoms of at-risk student behavior, and administrative staff should be responsive to their needs. It is especially important that teachers dealing with minority students have training in language and cultural differences. Schools need to be a model for equal opportunity and a place where the individual's needs for achievement and positive experiences can be met. The needs of minority students, low-income students, and students with special problems must be addressed.

What Kinds of Programs Help At-Risk Students?

Successful programs often separate at-risk students from other students, relate work to education, are small, have low student-to-teacher ratios, and provide counseling and supportive services. Most programs emphasize flexibility and tailor curriculum to the learning needs of the individual students. They are often innovative, providing alternatives to traditional promotion policies, structuring curriculum in nontraditional ways, offering early childhood education programs, and including vocational education in alternative settings.

Finally, effective programs are involved in a broad range of support services to help at-risk students improve their low self-esteem while providing a supportive system in which they can begin to have positive experiences. These include remediation programs, residential placement, substance abuse programs, alternative education placement, and close follow-up procedures on truancy issues.

Chapter Four

Oliver: At-Risk Adolescent Case Study

My youngest son, Oliver, provides us with an authentic first-hand experience with at-risk behaviors and the importance for schools to provide and monitor interventions that help to reduce the frequency of behavior incidents and/or to provide stabilization. From preschool through fifth grade, evaluation is difficult because little ones are developing into who they will become. It is in middle school that children show up as who they are, and their arrival may be accompanied with problems. The absence of adequate interventions and support to help with the problems is a malignancy that grows and spreads over time.

Oliver began stealing at age five. In kindergarten, I recalled organizing his little backpack, as I did almost every night, when I discovered a flyer from his teacher. It was a written plea for parents to check their child's backpack to see if there was a toy that they did not recognize. As with most backpacks, zippered compartments are every kid's fancy. So I opened each compartment, and guess what? There was a girl's toy in one of them. The story began with "it's mine" and ended with "she let me play with it."

Oliver is a stutterer. The more he lied, the more he stuttered. Of course I gave him the "you can't take things that do not belong to you;" and "how would you feel if it was your toy that someone took it?" lecture. He seemed puzzled by my scolding tone and attitude, but he showed remorse for his actions. This became a scene that would repeat itself over and over again. At first I thought that this was typical behavior that I could coach him out of, so I didn't panic. I took the toy to his class, gave it to his teacher, and shared the scene from the night before with her. His teacher also stated that she felt this was not unusual and agreed that we should not be concerned.

His teacher took that opportunity to tell me that she observed certain behaviors that may be signs that Oliver had a learning disability. For exam-

ple, he appeared to have delays in cognitive skills and grasping basic directives. She continued to explain that tests for special-education placements
were not administered until first grade. At first, I was saddened by her obser-
vations. But soon, the educator part of me kicked in and I felt a sense of
relief. As an educator, I knew that Oliver would be best served if he were
taught at his ability level. So again, I didn't panic, *yet*.

I had been an Internet shopper for many years. Oliver grew into that habit
as well. The only problem was he was shopping with *my* credit card and
without my knowledge! He must have studied my Internet habits long and
hard. He brings new meaning to the reality that children do as you do, not as
you say. At eight, he had mastered how to input the correct data: his name,
address, credit card number, and expiration date. Back then, the three- or
four-digit code on the front or back of cards did not exist. I think Oliver may
have been the driving force behind the use of codes to prevent identity theft.

Next, was the Palm Pilot fiasco. One day, I saw a medium-sized box on
the front porch. It was addressed to Oliver. I carefully opened the box before
calling Oliver to the kitchen. It was a Palm Pilot, which cost around $400.
"Oliver! Come here. What is this?" He looked at me as if I were crazy. "It's a
Palm Pilot, Mom." "Where did this come from?" I asked. His responses went
from his teacher must have sent it to him for his good grades, to neighbors
who had upgraded the Palm Pilot for their son bought him the older model.
Of course I gave him the "no one is going to purchase anything costing this
much money" speech.

Over the next few days, two more Palm Pilots arrived. The local post
office staff started to look at me strangely. Before returning all three Palm
Pilots, I had to plead to get those charges reversed. I told the credit card
companies that my credit card usage reflects my purchasing habits, and this
clearly contradicts my purchasing history. I further explained that my com-
puter-savvy eight-year-old made these unauthorized purchases. The companies agreed that the purchases within days of each other was a bit out of the
ordinary and advised me to hide my credit cards.

Around 1997, most adolescent boys and girls "needed" a scooter. I refused to buy into the scooter craze. I questioned their safety and their price.
With that said, when Oliver proudly announced that one of our neighbors
purchased a newer model scooter for their son, thus giving the older model to
Oliver, it was a believable explanation. The mother of the boy who owned
the scooter showed up at my door to cautiously inform me that other neighborhood kids told her that Oliver stole her son's scooter. Oliver lied, lied, and
lied. Then he finally admitted to stealing the scooter, and I began to panic.

This drove me to get online to locate psychologists who specialized in
working with children. As I read various doctors' profiles, I was trying to
match what I thought would be the right fit for Oliver. I thought Oliver would
speak more freely to a gentler, more compassionate doctor. So I chose a

female. She played nicely with Oliver. They played word games, number games, and mind games. None of the games addressed the stealing.

After three sessions of these play dates, she referred Oliver to a psychiatrist. He didn't play games with Oliver. He asked Oliver if he'd ever hurt animals, started fires, or run away from home. The answers were no, no, and no. He asked questions that led to answers that led him to diagnose Oliver as depressed. As a mother, I questioned what could have made Oliver depressed. I was the one who was depressed. I had an eight-year-old son who had been stealing and lying since age five. The psychiatrist prescribed Prozac and this marked the beginning of Oliver's introduction to psychotropic drugs.

Over the next three years, Prozac slowed Oliver's speech, but did nothing for his uncontrollable desire to steal. During the Christmas holiday at age nine, Oliver walked to the Kmart store located two blocks from our home. He returned some unwanted clothing, which left him with a large, empty shopping bag and money in his pocket. So, Oliver stuffed the bag with clothing and attempted to leave the store. At this point, the security guard ordered Oliver to stop. As a result of this incident, Oliver was fined restitution in the amount of $150.

The Kmart experience scared him enough to get through middle school without further legal issues. Incidents of theft continued periodically with the familiar scene of me investigating, providing consequences, returning stolen items, and asking God for help. Needless to say my family felt helpless. The at-risk characteristics previously explored became his behavior pattern beginning in Oliver's freshman year of high school and continued after graduation.

ADVERSITIES

After seventeen years of marriage, Oliver's father and I separated. Oliver, who was fifteen at the time, always loved to rearrange his bedroom furniture, so he was thrilled to relocate to a new community as he was starting high school; a new home, and a new life. However, I knew that separation anxiety might loom over Oliver from time to time, even though he assured me that he was fine with the fact that Mom and Dad will no longer live in the same house. He ran away from home a few times and I suspected it was to get extra attention from his father, but it didn't work. Each time he ran away, I was the one who was responsible for finding him and bringing him home.

EXPERIENCING LIMITED SUCCESS IN SCHOOL

Oliver's high school was a sprawling, impressive, state-of-the-art learning institution. With a student population of more than 2,500, they offered every extracurricular activity, sport, and club imaginable. Tryouts for basketball came in October and for the first time in a long time, Oliver was excited about school. During the second day of tryouts, he fractured his right leg and was unable to proceed with tryouts. The next day, he went into the school and walked right out. He ditched school repeatedly throughout his freshman year of high school.

UNINTERESTED IN SCHOOL ACTIVITIES

After the opportunity to try out for the basketball team was lost, school had become a dreaded thought every Sunday evening. Despite my encouragement to let the past remain the past and start fresh, Oliver was unwilling to attend or participate in any school-related event. By the second semester of his freshman year, he had begun to withdraw from friends who were successful in school. The friendships he retained were toxic and fed into his state of isolation and self-destruction.

LOW ACADEMIC ACHIEVERS

Oliver received special-education services for a learning disability since he was in first grade. He always struggled academically but it wasn't until high school that behavior issues escalated at both home and school. We thought maybe military school would be a viable option and reluctantly, Oliver agreed to try. While waiting for the aptitude test to be scored, we attended an orientation and toured the campus, only to learn the regretful news that he scored too low to be considered for admission.

IMPULSIVITY

By November of his freshman year, the novelty of his new school had diminished. Oliver's dean informed me that Oliver had been walking into school and walking right out, as evident from the camera videos. If he stayed in school on any given day, he would cut classes. He had been issued after-school detentions but refused to serve them. Upon learning this, I made an appointment for Oliver to be evaluated by a highly recommended psychologist. After three counseling sessions, Oliver was referred to a psychiatrist and placed on medication to help him control his impulsivity.

COURT INVOLVEMENT

Upon arriving home from work one day, the stench of marijuana greeted me at the door. Oliver was not at home. He had a curfew of 7:00 p.m. on school nights and 9:00 p.m. on the weekend. I received a call from the police department around 11:30 p.m., informing me that Oliver had been picked up and ticketed for consumption of alcohol. Oliver received probation for this ticket, marking my first of several trips to the police station and subsequent court appearances.

In the next incident, Oliver asked for permission to go out with some friends. I told him "no" because he continued to disobey house rules. He debated with me for about twenty minutes, kissed me on the cheek, and ran out of the house. He returned home at about 1:00 a.m. with his second ticket for alcohol consumption and a $75 fine. The next day was Saturday and as we dissected the events from the day before, with much deliberation and tears, Oliver told me that he had no idea why he repeatedly made negative, destructive choices.

TRUANCY

By the end of his freshman year, Oliver had accumulated nineteen truancies. The school failed to contact me to report his nonattendance. The next consequence was a Saturday detention. During his Saturday detention, he decided to smoke a cigarette in the washroom. He went to school on Monday and was suspended from school for four days. His performance at school and at home confirmed that he desperately needed increased supervision and structure.

MENTAL HEALTH DISORDERS

At the beginning of summer break, Oliver slept for fourteen hours straight. Concerned about what that may suggest, I took him to another psychiatrist for a consultation (He refused to cooperate with the previous one, stating that he felt she did not like him). From her evaluation, Oliver was diagnosed as severely depressed with bipolar disorder and she instructed me to take him to Linden Oaks Hospital for an extensive evaluation. He was placed in their therapeutic day-school for two weeks.

With a multitude of unresolved issues, Oliver reluctantly agreed to be placed in a residential facility for boys at the end of his freshman year in high school. The program was designed to help adolescent boys with anger management, problem solving, alcohol and drug education, relaxation, family dynamics, communication, and academic achievement. Clients were taught how to set goals and learn to make better choices.

Under the supervision of the group-home coordinator, each boy is given a treatment plan following an initial assessment. All treatment plans address individual needs based upon each boy's family history. Clients receive fifteen to twenty hours of group sessions per week, as well as individual therapy one to two times weekly or more if needed. Clients who were not admitted under court order could leave at any time. Oliver walked out of the residential home after a month and a half.

VICTIMIZATION

Oliver confessed to me that he had become involved in gang-initiation talks. Out of peer pressure and fear for the violent acts that he would be forced to commit, he was afraid to go to school. He stated that he was equally afraid to disassociate himself from the gang for fear of his own safety. In an attempt to keep him safe and in school, I requested an emergency individualized education program (IEP) review and the team determined that he would be better served in an alternate school placement. Oliver was involved in an altercation with a man hired to transport the students to and from the alternative school. The driver was fired for provoking a fight with a minor.

LOW SOCIOECONOMIC STATUS (SES)

Oliver did not live in an underresourced community. It was quite the opposite. But the community was a disadvantage for us because of its "boys will be boys" mentality. Entrenched in despair, I was vulnerable to whatever advice or support I received and had little means of evaluating its validity. It became evident that the empathy route created a sense of empowerment for Oliver, as he continued his reign of disobedience.

Clearly, Oliver possessed multiple at-risk traits that severely compromised his success in school. Remember, truancy is the umbrella that covers other at-risk behaviors. We are going to track Oliver's truancy behavior as we detail my comprehensive behavior system. Schools need to be on the frontline for students. It is incomprehensible how a student can be truant for nineteen days without the school informing the parent(s) and requiring official truancy support. Truancy opens the door for the kinds of at-risk behaviors that may be irreversible.

Chapter Five

The Behavior System

Schools need to be especially sensitive to the signs of violence and abuse and need to be on the frontline to protect all the students they serve. Students often experience many of the same traumatic experiences as adults. For example, some students may suffer violence by adults, relatives, and other students in their lives. They also may be plagued by an undiagnosed or untreated mental illness.

Many at-risk students come from homes where school policies are misunderstood or unappreciated. Students from such environments will frequently create situations that place home and school at odds with each other. This disconnection between home and school is the formula for failure that encourages student misconduct. The loss of trust in parents or teachers, the loss of innocence, and confusion to sort it all out can cause wounds that are difficult to understand and manage.

In an effort to create a positive school culture that promotes learning and achievement for at-risk students, I developed a comprehensive behavior system for the continuum of student growth and development. Barriers to student learning are quickly identified and addressed to help educators effectively monitor student misconduct. Educators will also be able to organize the educational structure of their school around this comprehensive behavior system that tracks a student's behavior in order to enlist the appropriate support or interventions and to become aligned for success.

Most schools publish an annual parent–student handbook that contains a section on student discipline. The student discipline policy may define behavior expectations and consequences for when the expectations are not followed. The consequences will demonstrate a succession of severity based upon the frequency of offenses. Most students and parents are not impacted by the policy because there will be minimal behavior infractions and the consequence(s) earned will eliminate future misconduct.

Students who demonstrate inappropriate at-risk behaviors may not respond to traditional discipline procedures and going through numerous steps or levels of misconduct prolongs the call for support and interventions needed to address the behaviors. This delay invites the potential for school violence and puts communities in crisis. My 3-Prong Behavior Map (figure 5.1) enables educators to quickly identify and address students who chronically misbehave in school.

1st Offense	2nd Offense	3rd Offense
Date _____ Time _____	Date _____ Time _____	Date _____ Time _____
Offense description:	Offense description:	Offense description:

➢ parent contact (method)
 	
➢ counsel/ mentor
 	
date _____
	➢ parent meeting date
	  _____
	
	➢ Saturday School
	  Detention(SSD)
	
	date _____
		➢ parent meeting date
		  _____
		
		➢ Saturday School Detention(
		  SSD)
		
		date _____
		➢ Student Advocacy Support
		  (SAS)
		
		date _____

Notes: Staff Signature	Notes: Staff Signature	Notes: Staff Signature

Figure 5.1.   3-Prong Behavior Map

SATURDAY SCHOOL DETENTION

The purpose for a Saturday School detention is to provide an additional intervention to address chronic minor behaviors that, if continued, will lead to an out-of-school suspension followed by an expulsion recommendation.

The goal of a Saturday School detention is to provide students with a pointed, focused research and writing assignment on the offense that brought them to this consequence. Students should leave a Saturday School detention with a clear understanding that the repetition of the behavior that caused the detention could lead to the worst consequence of all, expulsion.

Saturday School Detention Format:

SSD Format

- Minimum five hours of material that explores issues or interests leading to the offense
- One Saturday School reschedule allowed
- Recommended time: 9:00–noon
- No admittance after 9:05 a.m.
- A student may not serve more than two Saturday School detentions per semester
- Students are to write for the entire three hours
- No sleeping, reading, talking, or electronic use during Saturday School
- Inappropriate behaviors during or refusal to serve a Saturday School detention results in a suspension

Saturday School Detention Offenses:

Typical Saturday School Detention (SSD) Offenses

- Disruptive behavior (2nd–3rd offense)
- Disrespect toward school personnel
- Providing false evidence (2nd–3rd offense)
- Bullying (2nd–3rd offense)
- Improper internet use (2nd–3rd offense)
- Cheating (2nd–3rd offense)
- Theft (valued between $100–$300)*
- Threatening other students
- Provoking/ instigating a fight (2nd–3rd offense)
- Truancy (2nd–3rd offense)
- Tardy to school/ class (2nd–3rd offense)
- Gambling (2nd–3rd offense)
- Vandalism (valued between $100–$300)*
- Sexual harassment (1st–2nd offense)
- Weapon look-alikes (2nd–3rd offense)

- Drug look-alikes (2nd–3rd offense)
- Horse playing (2nd–3rd offense)

* Restitution required

STUDENT ADVOCACY SUPPORT

Student advocacy support (SAS) is introduced to provide additional support services, including a monitoring component, that can help those students who continue to repeat the same minor offense or a more significant offense to track their transformation. The services include: creating an individual service plan (ISP), coordinating life-skills groups/assemblies, facilitating wraparound services, recruiting and managing in-kind service providers, and partnering with community leaders to support student and family needs.

An ISP is not a special-education document. It may be used in conjunction with an IEP for students receiving special-education services, but it is a stand-alone form for students requiring SAS. The ISP provides the SAS team with a snapshot of what interventions the student needs, by whom, and a suggested timeline. The review process enables the team to monitor the student's progress and tweak it as needed.

Additional support services are enlisted for chronic or more severe behavior. This level of support is sometimes referred to as a wraparound service, an intensive, individualized care-management process for youth with serious or complex needs. Wraparound was initially developed in the 1980s as a means for maintaining youth with the most serious emotional and behavioral problems in their home and community. SAS should be implemented for more significant student behaviors, as seen in the following chart. SAS targets:

- Bullying
- Netiquette
- Sexting
- Violence awareness/prevention
- Drug and alcohol use/treatment
- Internship/apprentice opportunities
- Community service
- Abandonment
- Teen pregnancy
- Survival strategies
- Chronic truancy
- Court involvement
- Sexual harassment

The coordinated linking of school and community resources to support the needs of at-risk students and their families to address psychological, health, and social concerns is essential to improving situations that placed students at risk in the first place. Communities that have developed their own version of SAS must encompass wraparound services in order to support the transformation process of improving the lives of students and families who are at risk.

During the wraparound process, a team of individuals who are relevant to the well-being of the student collaboratively develops an individualized plan of care, implements this plan, and evaluates its success over time. The wraparound plan typically includes formal services and interventions, together with community services and interpersonal support and assistance provided by friends, relatives, and other people drawn from the family's social network. The team convenes frequently to measure the plan's components against relevant indicators of success. Plan components and strategies are revised when outcomes are not being achieved.

Wraparound services can be particularly useful for linking schools and community resources and integrating the efforts of high schools and their feeder middle schools. For example, in Oliver's case, his truancy warranted school and juvenile court support to get and keep him in school. Representatives from each resource form a council and this council helps coordinate and integrate programs serving the district. Leadership, communication, and maintenance become an ongoing development of a comprehensive continuum of programs and services.

One must never forget the need for wraparound services in crisis assistance and prevention. Schools must respond to minimize the impact of and prevent crises. This requires systematic programs for emergency response at the school level and community-wide, and minimizing risk factors to prevent crises related to violence, suicide, and child abuse. The council can take the lead in planning ways to prevent crises by developing programs for conflict mediation.

Collaborations involving school, home, and community have the potential for improving schools, strengthening neighborhoods, and leading to a marked reduction of at-risk students' problems. Comprehensive SAS partnerships represent a promising direction for efforts to generate essential interventions to address the barriers to effective teaching and learning. They broaden resources and strategies to enhance student support, which leads to student success. Such partnerships must also weave together resources and strategies to enhance communities that support all youth and their families and enable success at school and beyond.

After accepting support, parents must demonstrate consistency in the rehabilitation process. From the beginning, parents or other family members must rally around their child and provide a sense of purpose to make the

Sample Individual Service Plan (ISP)

Student: _____   Date: _____

Prepared By: _____   Title: _____

Grade: _____   Gender: _____

No.	Traits	RtI Ltr.	Supp. Docs Y / N	Target date	Review date	Outcome
1	Low academic achiever					
2	Limited success in school					
3	Uninterested in school…					
4	Impulsivity					
5	Family adversities					
6	Mental health disorders					
7	Victimization					
8	Truancy					
9	Low Socioeconomic…					
10	Court involved					
13						
14						
15						

RtI Resources

A.   Coordinate life-skills groups/ assemblies
B.   Facilitate wrap-around services
C.   Recruit and manage in-kind service providers
D.   Partner with community leaders to support student needs
E.   Referral for alternate placement
F.   Other _____

Outcomes

Recovered	Improved	Need Additional Support	On Target
(R)	(I)	(NAS)	(OT)

Figure 5.2.

recommended changes and take the prescribed steps to achieve recovery for the child and the family. Also, students need to accept responsibility for the choices they have made, accept support as given, fully participate in the rehabilitation process, and understand that change doesn't occur overnight.

In the next chapter, we look deeper into appropriate response to intervention strategies for the at-risk behaviors previously identified and provide the best practices needed to reverse the destructive paths many at-risk students take. As we explore the resources required to provide the recommended interventions, I encourage you to draft two columns on poster paper. The interventions that can be easily implemented go in column one. The ones that will require additional resources go in column two. Toward the bottom of the poster paper, draw a timeline indicating the intervention implementation process.

3-Prong Map	Out of School Suspension	Alternative Placement

Disruptive behavior
 	
Providing false evidence
 	
Bullying
 	
Improper internet use
 	
Inappropriate electronic use
 	
Cheating
 	
Theft *
 	
Provoking/ instigating a fight
 	
Truancy
 	
Tardy to school/ class
 	
Gambling
 	
Vandalism *
 	
Sexual harassment (1st offense)
 	
Weapon look-alikes
 	
Drug look-alikes
 	
Horse playing
 	
Disrespect toward staff
 	
Threatening other students
 	
Possession or use of matches/ lighter and/ or tobacco
	After 3rd offense on the 3-Prong Map or:
	
	Fighting on school campus
	
	Provoking a fight that leads to a fight
	
	Threatening school personnel
	
	Theft- ($100-$300) **
	
	Vandalism- ($100-$300) **
	
	Sexual harassment (2nd offense)
	
	First time possession or use of:
	
	Firecrackers/ poppers/alcohol
		After 10-day suspension or:
		
		Possession/consumption of:
		
		   · Alcohol (2nd offense)
		
		   · Cannabis **
		
		   · Other mind-altering drugs **
		
		Possession or use of:
		
		   · Knife **
		
		   · Gun/bb gun **
		
		   · Chemicals/explosives **
		
		Firecrackers/poppers- (2nd offense)
		
		Sexual harassment (3rd offense)**
		
		Assaulting school personnel
		
		Theft (valued over $300) **
		
		Chronic Truancy (after 3rd offense)
		
		Vandalism (valued over $300) **

	5-10 days	**1-2 semesters**

*restitution
**police intervention

Figure 5.3.

ESSENTIAL IDEAS TO REMEMBER

- The 3-Prong Behavior Map enables educators to quickly identify and address students who chronically misbehave in school.
- Saturday School Detention provides an additional intervention to address chronic minor behaviors that, if continued, will lead to an out-of-school suspension followed by an expulsion recommendation. Students should leave a Saturday School detention with a clear understanding that the repetition of the behavior that caused the detention could lead to the worst consequence of all, expulsion.
- Student advocacy support (SAS) provides students who continue to repeat the same minor offense or a more significant offense with additional support services that have a monitoring component to help them track their transformation.
- Individual service plan (ISP) coordinates life-skills groups/assemblies, facilitating wraparound services, recruiting and managing in-kind service providers, and partnering with community leaders to support student and family needs.
- Linking of school and community resources is a critical component to supporting the needs of at-risk students and their families. The psychological, health, and social concerns essential to improving situations that placed students at risk must be addressed.
- A wraparound service is a team of individuals who are relevant to the well-being of the student that collaboratively develops an individualized plan of care, implements this plan, and evaluates success over time. Wraparound services can be particularly useful for linking schools and community resources and integrating the efforts of high schools and their feeder middle schools.
- Collaborations involving school, home, and community have the potential for improving schools, strengthening neighborhood, and leading to a marked reduction of at-risk students' problems.
- Comprehensive SAS partnerships represent a promising direction for efforts to generate essential interventions to address the barriers to effective teaching and learning.

Chapter Six

Response to Intervention

Response to Intervention (RtI) marginally combats the phenomenon that we undertake daily to meet the needs of three groups of learners. In the first group, Tier 1 students receive research-based, high-quality general education that incorporates ongoing screening, progress monitoring, and prescriptive assessment to design instruction. Expectations are taught, reinforced, and monitored in all settings by all adults. Discipline and other data inform the design of interventions that are preventative and proactive. This group receives general or universal instruction in large and small group settings.

The teaching staff must receive sufficient and ongoing professional development to deliver the Tier 1 core instructional program in the way it was designed. The expectation is that if the Tier 1 program is implemented with a high degree of integrity and by highly trained teachers, then most of the students receiving this instruction will show outcomes upon assessment that indicate a level of proficiency that meets minimal benchmarks for performance in the skill area.

In the second group, Tier 2 interventions are provided to students at risk of academic or social challenges and students identified as underachieving who require specific supports to make sufficient progress in general education. They are often straddling between averages, creating fluctuating benchmark scores. The intervention level for this group of students may be referred to as strategic.

For the third group, Tier 3 interventions are provided to students with intensive/chronic academic or behavior needs based on ongoing progress monitoring and diagnostic assessment. RtI has the flexibility of allowing the school to establish the level of progress monitoring that is both feasible, given the instructional or social demands of the classroom, and meaningful in obtaining knowledge and growth of a student's response to instruction.

Schools are challenged to quickly locate the trigger(s) that plague students' ability to be successful and provide the appropriate remedy. RtI serves as the framework which supports the platform of direct services to combat problematic behaviors and deficiencies. The marked difference between RtI practices for at-risk students and their counterparts is the individual service plan discussed in chapter 3. It is critical that at-risk students be monitored with fidelity in order to achieve a positive change in their behavior and academic success. Let's examine specific strategies and provide school districts with the appropriate remedy for each at-risk behavior previously identified.

EXPERIENCING LIMITED SUCCESS IN SCHOOL

Today's classrooms include student populations that are increasingly diverse and many students may not be experiencing success in school. These populations include children who fall outside of the mainstream. For example, recent immigrants, children with physical handicaps, Latinos, African Americans, and definitely at-risk students comprise today's typical classroom. Schools must take the challenge and provide a realistic pathway for at-risk students to achieve success. The reality of students feeling unsuccessful in many urban schools is a result of low expectations for them.

Remedy: Schools educating at-risk students must hire the most dedicated and caring staff in order to replenish the lack of feeling successful in school. The staff must be trained in best practices for educating at-risk students, such as:

- Build positive relationships with the students. Get to know their likes and dislikes, their family life, and their ability levels. It is crucial that all students know their teacher cares about them.
- Allow students to work on more hands-on activities, projects, and active participation. Diminish the use of worksheets and workbooks.
- Find out what interests the students have and encourage them to read and write about their interests. Providing greater choice in what students read and write will increase literacy skills.
- Work with at-risk students in small, supportive groups where they are taught at their instructional level. Frequently monitor and access progress so the instruction matches the needs of the child.
- Maintain high expectations for all students. At-risk students need to be appropriately challenged and encouraged with the words, "You are smart! You can do it!"

LOW ACADEMIC ACHIEVERS

There is a correlation between students identified as low achievers and living in poverty. The damaging effects of poverty on at-risk students have been well documented. Numerous studies have shown poverty to be highly correlated with poor performance in academics, lower IQ scores, and an increased risk of dropping out of school. Schools are limited in effecting change in the lifestyle of the students, yet they are responsible for providing them with an education appropriate to their needs.

Nonpoverty students may also be at risk of experiencing low academic achievement. The reasons are varied and random, and therefore multiple testing instruments may be necessary in order to provide the answers and the plan to get the student on or near grade level. The ISP should include the necessary resources to execute the plan. It may contain wraparound services such as counseling, tutoring, and mentoring.

Remedy: Schools educating at-risk students must hire teachers with substantive content knowledge and above-average pedagogical skills to meet students' academic and behavior needs.

TRUANCY

Any unexcused absence from school is considered truancy, but states enact their own school-attendance laws. State law determines the age at which a child is required to begin attending school, the age at which a child may legally drop out of school, and the number of unexcused absences that constitutes legally truancy. Truancy has been clearly identified as one of the early warning signs of students headed for potential delinquent activity. Engaging at-risk students has been identified as one key element in preventing truancy.

It is critically important to identify those who have disengaged and provide support for reengagement. This process includes clarifying and bringing into the open the negative perceptions of school that students hold, reframing school learning in a meaningful and concrete way, renegotiating students' involvement in school learning, and establishing a productive working relationship. Most truancy-reduction efforts can be categorized as school-based, court-based, or community-based.

School-based: Truancy programs in schools aim to identify truancy and attendance problems before they reach a chronic level and before patterns become entrenched and harder to reverse. The first step is to develop a school-based mentoring program. Truancy mentors should work on academics and/or assist with homework with their mentees. They need to develop collaborative relationships with teachers in order to enhance overall educational achievement. The goal of a truancy mentoring program is to redirect negative habits by developing healthy ones and to provide positive adult support, thereby reducing risk factors that result in truancy.

Community-based: Community-based programs recognize that truancy is not an individual or family problem alone, but that chronic truancy is a community problem that can best be addressed by collaboration among various systems within the community. Their objective is to reduce juvenile crime, loitering, graffiti, and the number of children unsupervised in the community. Full implementation involves a commitment of school principals, parents or guardians, community liaisons, and police officers.

"Student Welfare and Attendance (SWAT)," a truant recovery program in Richmond, California, is one example of a community-based approach. It is a collaborative effort between the school district and all community police jurisdictions within its boundaries. The program is preventive rather than punitive. Its primary task is to return truant students to school as soon as possible. The program operates under the authority of the school's office personnel.

SWAT authorizes the local police jurisdictions to make contact with students on the streets during school hours. Students without a valid excuse slip are taken into temporary custody and transported to the SWAT office for processing. SWAT personnel attempt to contact the youth's parents for a face-to-face meeting, in which both can be counseled and the parent can return the child to school. If a parent cannot be reached, SWAT personnel will return the youth to school. The school site is also contacted, and both the school and the SWAT office closely monitor the student's attendance in the future.

Court-based: Court-based programs leverage the power of the court to coordinate and oversee the delivery of services that are identified for the truant youth, and often for the family as well. Programs can differ in how long they run, the number of times the youth/family appears before the judge, the role of a social worker or case manager, the representatives included, and the types of services overseen by the court.

Many systems have established diversion programs, which are designed to include relief to the courts, police department, and probation office; and to provide better outcomes for the offender after a petition has been received, but before adjudication. Court-based programs involve school and community support by providing attendance workshops that are alternatives to standard truancy court hearings, and truancy case managers. Factors contributing to truancy stem from four realms: school, home, community, and personal characteristics.

School Factors

- Lack of effective and consistently applied attendance policies

- Poor record-keeping, making truancy difficult to spot
- Suspension as a punishment for truancy
- Automatic "Fs" for poor attendance
- Parents/guardians not notified of absences
- Uncaring teachers
- Unwelcoming atmosphere
- Unsafe environment
- Inadequate identification of special-education needs

Home Factors

- Family adversities
- Victim of abuse or neglect
- Pressures arising from teen pregnancy or parenting
- Parental alcoholism or drug abuse
- Parents/guardians who do not value education and are complacent in the child's absences

Community Factors

- Safety issues such as violence near home or between home and school
- Negative role models, such as peers who are truant or delinquent

Personal Factors

- Poor academic performance
- Unmet special education needs
- Lack of self-esteem
- Unmet mental health needs
- Alcohol and drug use and abuse
- Lack of vision of education as a means to achieve goals

Remedy: Adopt policies that support a comprehensive truancy-reduction program to achieve positive outcomes. For instance, in-school suspension policies, detention, and use of alternative school programs each allow students to continue academic progress in the school setting rather than having unsupervised time outside of school. Effective truancy-reduction programs must contain the following components:

- Whole family involvement
- A continuum of supports, including meaningful incentives for good attendance and consequences for poor attendance

- Collaboration among community law enforcement, mental health workers, mentors, and social service providers, in addition to educators
- Concrete and measurable goals for program performance and student performance
- Good record keeping and ongoing evaluation of progress toward those goals

UNINTERESTED IN SCHOOL ACTIVITIES

Many students in their preteen through teen years are bored because school no longer challenges them. Middle-school students are often off task in school due to daydreaming about their upcoming teen years. High-school students struggle with the difference between perception and reality. If you add any at-risk characteristic to the equation, the challenge to engage them becomes more difficult. Nonetheless, all students can be engaged with the right strategies and techniques. There are several things that can be done to engage students. The following are examples of some of the strategies:

Challenge students. Design activities with some difficulty that require active learning to keep them interested. Instead of asking students to write a simple book report, for instance, give them a statement of an ethical position and have them write an argument for or against it based on the book. Better yet, have your students write their report in the same narrative style as the book they are writing about.

Use visual and multimedia support. If there's one thing young adolescents dislike, it's being lectured to. Instead of simply presenting material orally, make ample use of visual aids. If you are teaching a history lesson, find images on the web that illustrate the point you are making. If your activity involves learning about the Harlem Renaissance, for example, bring in some song clips from the jazz era. Encourage or require students to do the same when they make oral presentations.

Welcome wrong answers. Students of middle-school age generally dislike having their ideas shot down. Being told he is wrong once can discourage a preteen from raising ideas again. If your classroom activity involves soliciting answers to a question, pursue the thinking behind answers that are not correct. Without singling out a student, ask the class why these kinds of answers are so common. Bring in examples of famously intelligent people who have been wrong in the past. You might even try soliciting a series of wrong answers on purpose before asking for the right answer.

Encourage group work. Group work is an effective way to get students who crave social interaction to focus on educational material while chatting with their friends. Get creative and bold with group work.

Instead of teaching a math lesson, make it a group activity. Have students read a chapter in your textbook individually, and then come together in small groups to teach each other. Encourage them to ask questions of each other in a respectful way.

Enhance student learning with quality, not quantity. Many new teachers focus on quantity, rather than quality. That is, they feel they must "cover" everything mapped out on curriculum guides. They at times resort to a teacher-centered approach with lecture as the primary means of delivery because it seems the most expeditious. The problem is that, with instruction like this, many students experience the content on a superficial level and don't fully comprehend it. Remember, curricular choices are to some extent made by the teacher. Focusing on content delivery, rather than actual student learning, is a disservice to teaching and learning.

Encourage student learning with depth, not breadth. Because teachers sometimes feel rushed to impart knowledge, they often make decisions that minimize student-centered discovery learning or cooperative activities—especially in high school. Teachers may feel that they "don't have time" to follow through with a planned group activity. They may categorize the act of playing a song for the class that relates to a specific piece of literature as "enrichment" that doesn't necessarily meet a specific learning objective. However, these valuable activities create meaningful connections for students, which foster motivation.

Encourage teachers to consider delving deeper into a topic and approach it from multiple perspectives. Try constructing a variety of student-centered activities that actively engage students. You may find that you cover less content, but the benefit of increased student learning and engagement balances the loss. Understanding how to maximize opportunities for student-centered learning in your high-school classroom is an ongoing challenge. Teaching students to approach a topic from a variety of perspectives and understand new layers of meaning is not always an easy task.

Remedy: Provide students with a deeper understanding of content to enhance their appreciation for learning. By using a student-centered approach, you will help all students to yearn to learn.

ADVERSITIES

Every one of us faces trials in our lives. Some face minimum hardships, while others may have serious adversities to overcome. Today, many families are faced with various types of adversities that affect the entire family unit. At-risk students often have fewer resources and limited support during difficult times. What are the steps to draw a more unified front and face these adversities as a family? In what ways can the family use these times of crisis to build better relationships and opportunities within their family?

Remedy: Implement wraparound services to provide a link between family adversity and the at-risk student and family. This is where open communication must take place, along with active listening skills in order to understand how the situation affects everyone.

MENTAL HEALTH DISORDERS

Preteens and teens can feel stressed about all types of issues, ranging from family problems to school pressures and relationship struggles. While many of these problems typify teen life, at-risk students, their parents, and other concerned adults may struggle with telling the difference between normal teen angst and the symptoms of mental problems. At-risk teen mental health issues can have more profound implications than simply making your teen seem grumpy and sullen.

While teens may initially drink or use illegal drugs due to peer pressure or curiosity, substance abuse can lead to an additional set of problems that complicate the treatment of any mental issue or illness. Columbine High School, Virginia Tech, Northern Illinois University, and Sandy Hook Elementary have educated us on the devastation of undetected or improperly treated mental illness. Here are some examples of situations or stressors that can lead to a mental health crisis:

Home or Environmental Triggers

- Changes to family structure: parents separate, divorce, or remarry
- Loss of any kind, such as a family member or friend due to death or relocation
- Loss of family pet
- Transitions between parents' homes
- Strained relationships with step-siblings or step-parents
- Changes in friendships
- Fights or arguments with siblings or friends
- Conflict or arguments with parents

School Triggers

- Worrying about tests and grades
- Overwhelmed by homework or projects

- Feeling singled out by peers or feelings of loneliness
- Pressures at school such as transitions between classes and school activities
- Bullying at school
- Pressure by peers
- Suspensions, detentions, or other discipline
- Use of seclusion or restraints
- Teachers who may not understand a symptom of their mental illness

Other Triggers

- Stops taking medication or misses a few doses
- Starts new medication or new dosage of current medication
- Medication stops working
- Use of drugs or alcohol abuse
- Pending court dates
- Being in crowds/large groups of people
- Changes in relationship with boyfriend, girlfriend, partner

Sometimes educators, families, or caregivers observe changes in a child's behavior that may indicate a crisis may be impending while other times the crisis occurs suddenly and without warning. You may be able to de-escalate or prevent a crisis from happening by identifying the early changes in behavior, an unusual reaction to daily tasks, an increase in their stress level, and so on. Here are some warning signs of a mental health crisis:

Inability to Cope with Daily Tasks

- Doesn't bathe, brush teeth, comb/brush hair
- Refuses to eat or eats too much
- Sleeps all day or refuses to get out of bed
- Doesn't sleep

Rapid Mood Swings

- Increase in energy
- Inability to stay still, pacing
- Depressed mood

Increased Agitation

- Makes verbal threats

- Violent, out-of-control behavior
- Destroys property
- Cruel to animals

Displays Abusive Behavior

- Hurting others
- Cutting self
- Alcohol or substance abuse

Loses Touch with Reality (Psychosis)

- Unable to recognize family or friends
- Confused thinking, strange ideas
- Thinking they are someone they are not
- Not understanding what people are saying

Isolation from School, Family, Friends

- No or little interest in extracurricular activities
- Changes in friendships
- Stops attending school, stops doing homework

Unexplained Physical Symptoms

- Eyes or facial expressions look different
- Increase in headaches, stomach aches
- Complains of not feeling well

When a mental health crisis or behavioral emergency occurs, untrained staff may not know what to do. A crisis can occur even when de-escalation techniques are used, and it's often nobody's fault. Children's behaviors and crisis situations can be unpredictable and occur without warning. If you are worried that a child is in or nearing a crisis, you can seek help in a number of ways. Before choosing which option to pursue, assess the situation. Consider whether the child is in danger of hurting themselves, others, or property.

Children cannot always communicate their thoughts, feelings, or emotions clearly or understand what others are saying to them during a crisis. As a first responder, and teachers and administrators certainly serve as first responders, it is important to empathize with the child's feelings, help de-escalate the crisis, and to assess the situation to determine if you need emergency assistance, guidance, or additional support. Seek outside resources or help when your actions are not helping. Here are some de-escalation techniques that may help resolve a crisis:

* Keep your voice calm
* Use short sentences
* Listen to his or her story
* Offer options instead of trying to take control
* Ask how you can help
* Remain calm and avoid overreacting
* Move slowly
* Don't argue or shout
* Express support and concern
* Keep stimulation level low
* Avoid eye contact/touching
* Be patient and accepting
* Announce actions before initiating them
* Give the person space, don't make him or her feel trapped

Remedy: If unable to defuse the crisis, quickly seek professional help. Trained mental health professionals can assess a child to determine the level of crisis intervention required and may refer families to short-term crisis stabilization services or hospitalization if appropriate.

IMPULSIVITY

Impulsivity is the general term used to describe a tendency to act quickly, often without thinking or caring about the consequences. To understand impulsivity, it is important to understand the word "impulse," which can be used in two different, although related, ways. With regard to behavior, an impulse is a sudden, strong, even irrational urge, desire, or action resulting from a particular feeling or state of mind. Within the central nervous system, a nerve impulse is the electrical and chemical process by which messages are sent along the nerves.

As a normal trait, one person may be more impulsive than another. For some, overly impulsive behavior lasts into later childhood, the teenage years, and even adulthood. Too much impulsivity, or not enough impulse control, can lead to behavior problems or unsafe actions. For example, children might impulsively run into a busy street without looking, grab a toy from another child, hit others, throw things, or behave in other inappropriate ways. All children may act this way from time to time, but overly impulsive children repeat these behaviors again and again, even after numerous warnings from parents, teachers, and other adults.

Preteens and teens who lack impulse control may blurt out hurtful comments, not finish projects, have trouble listening, interrupt others frequently, or hit others when they're angry. A pattern of such behavior can be a symptom of a behavior disorder. For instance, a greater than normal level of impulsivity is associated with the condition known as attention deficit hyperactivity disorder (ADHD). ADHD is characterized by greater than normal levels of impulsivity, hyperactivity, and distractibility. The following behaviors are classified as impulse-control disorders. They include:

- Intermittent explosive disorder: A pattern of behavior in which a person has trouble resisting aggressive impulses, resulting in sudden and severe outbursts of anger, violence, or destruction of property. The person may respond very aggressively to minor sources of stress or frustration. Because people can act aggressively for many different reasons, however, this condition is only diagnosed when the explosive behavior does not stem from another mental disorder, a medical condition, or a drug or medication.
- Kleptomania: An abnormal, uncontrollable, and repeated urge to steal. Often, objects are not taken because of their monetary value or because the person needs them, but because the objects have some kind of symbolic meaning for the person.
- Pyromania: An uncontrollable urge to set fires. The person usually feels tension while setting the fire, followed by pleasure while watching the fire burn.
- Trichotillomania: An irresistible urge to pull out one's hair, eyelashes, or eyebrows.

Remedy: Keep communication lines open and discuss the student's behaviors and feelings, not the adult team members'. While setting boundaries is important, remain calm and refrain from criticism. Trust your instincts and proactively invoke professional assistance when appropriate.

COURT INVOLVEMENT

Court-involved youth are youth who come in contact with the juvenile justice system for committing a status offense or a delinquent act. This automatically invokes the label of "at risk." Often disenfranchised by the education system and under juvenile justice system jurisdiction, these youth find it difficult to learn marketable skills or compete for jobs. The link between crime and lack of economic opportunity requires collaboration between employers, the juvenile justice system, and the workforce-development system.

To help develop effective strategies for improving vocational training, reducing youth crime, and recidivism, the team must:

- Understand the diverse needs of court-involved youth;
- Identify the most promising mix of employment and training strategies to move court-involved youth into the mainstream;
- Define the roles and responsibilities of the agencies and organizations that work with court-involved youth to enhance training and employment opportunities; and
- Recommend ways the workforce development, juvenile justice, education, social service, community-based support, and labor-market systems can collaborate to provide effective job training and employment for court-involved youth.

Promising programs challenge both policy makers and service providers to implement processes that prepare court-involved youth for jobs while also meeting developmental needs of youth, labor-market requirements of employers, and safety and security needs of communities. Programs that serve court-involved youth can be divided into three categories: early intervention, residential, and aftercare.

Early-Intervention Programs

Early-intervention programs are typically designed as prevention programs, either to divert youth from entering the juvenile justice system or to prevent youth from continuing their involvement with the system. The most effective early-intervention programs use a variety of approaches, including mentoring, afterschool support, employment and training, school-to-work, and college-access services. Intermediaries, such as community-based organizations, nonprofits, and job brokers, can provide consistent contacts for court-involved youth who are in the juvenile justice system or returning to the community after confinement.

Residential Programs

Court-sentenced youth may be committed to a residential facility due to mental health issues or a threat to public safety. Effective residential employment and training programs include those that operate on business sites and employ youth at competitive wages, engage youth in community service and restitution projects, prepare youth for employment using an entrepreneurship or a service-learning model, or train youth for specific jobs using industry-approved curriculums. These programs enable youth to develop practical skills they can use in the workforce after their release from residential facilities.

Aftercare Programs

Following their release from residential facilities, youth often remain the responsibility of the state juvenile justice or corrections agency and continue to require support services. Aftercare can provide critical services and support a youth's reintegration into the community. Aftercare programs that emphasize employment and training tend to be most effective when youth are in the community, are of legal working age, and have benefited from earlier services, such as counseling, basic skills, and interpersonal skills development.

The most effective aftercare programs typically involve formal partnerships between the juvenile justice system and other institutions or organizations. Some programs direct court-involved youth to employment and training programs, create and tailor slots for court-involved youth in job-training programs, or impart academic skills and knowledge through practical applications and "real work" projects. These programs create support networks that help youth develop appropriate attitudes and behaviors for participation in the community and the workforce.

There are six primary systems that affect court-involved youth: juvenile justice, workforce development, education, social services, community-based organizations, and the labor market. Effective job preparation requires the engagement of each of these systems. Enhancing collaboration, improving communication, and increasing the various systems' knowledge of each other are among the challenges confronted by policy makers, program personnel, and court-involved youth.

Remedy: Develop ongoing partnerships with agencies that maintain age-appropriate and comprehensive programs that require adult advocates and family participation. Work-based learning, academic development, job placement, and long-term follow-up are essential for measuring success.

VICTIMIZATION

The most common form of peer victimization is bullying, which typically involves a power imbalance where one child is (often repeatedly) hurt by one or more powerful students. Harm can result from physical bullying, such as hitting and shoving; verbal abuse in the form of insults or threats; or social bullying in which students spread mean rumors about other students, or openly exclude them from a group. Spreading malicious intent through social networks such as Facebook, Twitter, or text messages is called cyber-bullying. This form of bullying can be harmful and requires immediate attention.

Bullying is especially prevalent and damaging in middle school, as during this time children are defining themselves and establishing self-esteem, both of which will impact their future adult life. They are also more vulnerable to peer-rejection because needs for belonging and intimacy may be especially strong during early adolescence, when children are working to solidify their peer groups.

To account for the difference in the severity of negative outcomes as a result of peer victimization, I suggest schools encourage students to do a self-evaluation to determine their own perceived worth. It is vital that they feel desirable and competent in order for them to maintain a positive self-image. Accordingly, they should feel less threatened by others' evaluations of them. When thinking about self-evaluation, positive role models should affect the degree to which teens and young adults base their self appraisals on peer judgments, determining whether negative peer approval undermines their well-being.

Awareness and positive action can significantly reduce victimization. Schools should have a zero-tolerance antibullying policy. School policy and consequences should be visibly posted throughout the building. Also, schools should discourage any and all property exchange among students. Noncompliance should be treated as extortion. Finally, frequently remind parents and students of the depth of bullying behavior.

Remedy: Provide disciplinary consequences from counseling to alternate placement for noncompliance of the bullying policy. Suspensions are discouraged as they rarely eliminate victimization behavior.

LOW SOCIOECONOMIC STATUS

Socioeconomic status (SES) is often measured as a combination of education, income, and occupation. It is commonly conceptualized as the social standing or class of an individual or group. When viewed through a social-class lens, privilege, power, and control are emphasized. Inadequate education and increased dropout rates affect children's academic achievement, perpetuating the low SES status of the community.

The reality of low achievement levels in many urban schools is often a result of low expectations for students. Schools in low-SES communities suffer from high levels of unemployment, migration of the best qualified teachers, and low educational achievement. Poor academic performance often leads to diminished expectations, which spread across the board and undermine children's overall self-esteem.

The dramatic socioeconomic divide in education doesn't help matters. High-poverty, high-minority schools receive significantly less state and local money than do more prosperous schools, and students in such schools are more likely to be taught by teachers who are inexperienced or teaching outside their specialties. A teacher's years of experience and quality of training is correlated with children's academic achievement. Yet, children in low-income schools are less likely to have well-qualified teachers.

Also, low-SES students' inability to respond appropriately to adversity is a detriment to their school performance. For example, students with emotional issues may get so easily frustrated that they give up on a task when success was just moments away. Social dysfunction may inhibit a student's ability to work well in cooperative groups, quite possibly leading to his or her exclusion by group members who believe he or she isn't "doing their part." This exclusion and the accompanying decrease in collaboration and exchange of information exacerbate at-risk students' already shaky academic performance and behavior.

Strong, secure relationships help stabilize at-risk children's behavior and provide the core guidance needed to build lifelong social skills. Children who grow up with such relationships learn healthy, appropriate emotional responses to everyday situations. We will explore three factors, which serve as SES indicators: emotional and social challenges, acute and chronic stressors, and safety and health issues.

Emotional and Social Challenges

Some teachers may interpret students' emotional and social deficits as a lack of respect or manners, but it is more accurate and helpful to understand that some students come to school with a narrower range of appropriate emotional responses than we expect. The truth is that many children simply don't have the repertoire of appropriately acceptable responses. The proper way to deal with such a deficit is first to understand students' behavior and then to lay out clear behavioral expectations without sarcasm or resentment. Understand that children raised in poverty are more likely to display:

- "Acting-out" behaviors
- Impatience and impulsivity
- Gaps in politeness and social graces
- A more limited range of behavioral responses
- Inappropriate emotional responses
- Less empathy for others' misfortunes

These behaviors will likely puzzle, frustrate, or irritate teachers who have less experience teaching students raised in poverty, but it's important to avoid labeling, demeaning, or blaming students. It is much easier to condemn a student's behavior and demand that he or she change it than it is to help the student change it. Every proper response that you don't see at your school is one that you need to be teaching.

Cooperation, patience, embarrassment, empathy, gratitude, and forgiveness are crucial to a smoothly running, complex social environment (like a classroom). When students lack these positive attributes, teachers who expect humility or penitence may get a smirk instead, a response that may lead teachers to believe the student has an "attitude." It's the primary caregiver's job to teach the child appropriate responses, but when students do not bring these attributes to school, the school must teach them. What all students require:

1. Students need a primary safe and reliable relationship. Students would prefer parents, positive friends, and teachers, but may befriend someone who pays them a little attention. The relationships that teachers build with students form the single strongest access to student goals, motivation, and academic performance. For your school to foster high achievement, every student needs a reliable relationship.
2. Socialization is the drive for acceptance that encourages students to imitate their peers and join groups, from clubs to cliques to gangs. Students want to belong somewhere. Evidence suggests that it is peers, not parents, who have the greatest influence on school-age students. If your school aims to improve student achievement, academic success must be culturally acceptable among all students. Informally, teachers can incorporate classroom strategies that build relationships, strengthen peer acceptance, and foster social skills in class.

Acute and Chronic Stressors

Chronic stress has an insidious effect on learning and behavior, and you should recognize the symptoms in the classroom. A child who comes from a stressful home environment tends to channel that stress into disruptive behavior at school and be less able to develop a healthy social and academic life. Impulsivity, for example, is a common disruptive classroom behavior among low-SES students. But it's actually an exaggerated response to stress that serves as a survival mechanism: in conditions of poverty, those most likely to survive are those who have an exaggerated stress response.

Low-SES students are especially subject to stressors that undermine school behavior and academic performance. For example, transiency impairs students' ability to succeed in school and engage in positive social interactions. Whereas middle-class families usually move for social or economic improvement, the moves of low-income households are typically not voluntary. These moves compound the students' stress load by disrupting their social and academic lives.

Health and Safety Issues

Students who worry about safety concerns also tend to underperform academically. Exposure to community violence, an unsafe home, or a dangerous path to and from school contributes to lower academic performance. In addition, stress resulting from bullying and school violence impairs test scores, diminishes attention spans, and increases truancy. It is discouraging, but many high-school students either stay home or skip classes due to fear of violence.

Remedy: Invoke collaborative resources that directly improve the quality of students' lives living in low-SES communities.

In summary, truancy can create the onset of other at-risk behaviors. Experiencing limited success in school often contributes to at-risk students dropping out of school. Low academic achievement and declining interest in school activities frequently morphs into low self-esteem. Impulsivity produces problematic relationships. Adversities, mental health disorders, victimization, and court involvement negatively impact students and hinder their success in school. Finally, impoverished school communities serve to reinforce hopelessness. Schools must take the challenge to stop teaching subjects and start teaching children.

ESSENTIAL IDEAS TO REMEMBER

Success in school requires supporting the whole child. To succeed in school, students need strong leadership, effective instruction, high expectations, and elements that build trusting relationships. They also need a comprehensive program of academic and social support, including student advocacy support. Such support will ensure that at-risk students experience schools as supporting communities, enabling their success and not as environments of alienation and hostility. Too often, many at-risk children require a support system as a prerequisite to basic educational success.

Social and health-care services should be entwined with early learning opportunities. Children should be assessed on their strengths and weaknesses, so teachers will know how to better individualize instruction. Students needing consistent student advocacy support—beginning in elementary school—should continue through high school. Especially for students whose parents are at risk, learning how to navigate between school and home is a critical skill. Additionally, going through elementary to high school is for many students the final in a series of critical transitions for which they need guidance.

Teachers need to be strong communicators and actively engaged in reaching out to and building relationships with families in crisis. More teachers and administrators of diverse backgrounds are needed to better communicate with families and advocate for diverse students. Teachers must partner with students and community advocates to keep students safe. They need to listen to parent feedback, and be passionate advocates for their students.

We should add supports for at-risk students that build the awareness and knowledge of postsecondary opportunities, including navigating college-entrance requirements and building a high-school transcript that reflects readiness for advanced studies. At-risk students require special assistance to consider their possible future, especially those who will be the first generation of their families to engage in higher education. These are issues of teacher-to-student and teacher-to-family communications. By starting earlier and being consistent in communications about lifelong expectations, more at-risk students will have greater opportunities beyond high school.

Schools that succeed in involving families and community share two key practices. They focus on building trusting collaborative relationships among teachers, families, and community members and they embrace a philosophy of partnership where power and responsibility are shared. When families and community are involved, at-risk students do better in school. Family and community support increases student achievement, regardless of their economic, racial/ethnic, and educational background. Students are more likely to:

- Earn high grades and test scores, and enroll in higher-level programs
- Be promoted, pass their classes, and earn credits
- Attend school regularly
- Have better social skills, show improved behavior, and adapt well to school
- Graduate and go on to postsecondary education

Chapter Seven

Departmentalized versus School-within-a-School

Many at-risk students attend large or departmentalized schools, where they receive daily instruction from several different teachers. Research indicates students from such environments frequently create situations that place home and school at odds with each other. This home–school disconnection is the formula for failure that encourages students to seek alternative choices instead of attending school.

Most American middle and high schools, and many elementary schools, are departmentalized. Students receive daily instruction from several different teachers because each teacher specializes in a single subject. This practice is nearly universal in high schools and almost as common in the middle grades; it is often reinforced by certification regulations that stipulate only specialized teachers may be used in the secondary grades.

The rationale for such regulations is that the instructional content of each academic subject in the secondary grades requires teachers who are experts in the area, and that instruction is of higher quality when teachers can take special pride in their subject-matter discipline and can concentrate on preparing a limited number of outstanding lessons each day that are offered to several different classes. A teacher who provides daily instruction to several different classes decreases the opportunity to build positive relationships with those students who need stability and consistency in order sustain themselves and achieve in school.

Students who change teachers for each period of the day typically do not develop strong relationships as they can in earlier grades when there is only one instructor in their class. In the earlier grades, teachers are likely to adopt a student-orientation approach in which they take a broad view of the education of the whole child and assume a personal responsibility for the success of each individual in their class.

On the other hand, teachers in the departmentalized setting of later grades are more likely to take on a subject-matter approach. These teachers tend to have a professional identity with others in their field, and may seek to maintain higher standards in their teaching and expectations for student performance that may detract from their feelings of personal responsibility for student success. Research indicates at-risk students in these types of settings tend to feel more alienated from both teachers and peers. This feeling of alienation often leads to discipline problems.

Students in middle and high school are finding their identity, dealing with hormonal changes, and working through self-esteem issues. Instead of being uplifted and encouraged by a student-orientation approach, they are made to feel invisible and unimportant by the subject-matter approach. For the child who is already at risk due to other factors, this change in the teachers' approach can be particularly detrimental.

So how do we fix this dilemma? Two structural approaches may help to offset the negative effects of departmentalized staffing. The first is a form of semidepartmentalization in which the number of different specialized teachers assigned to each student in middle and secondary grades is limited. Analysis of national middle-school data indicates that semidepartmentalization promotes a more positive teacher–student climate than fully departmentalized schools, but precautions may be needed to ensure that high-quality instruction is still provided in each subject area.

Another way to offset the negative effects of departmentalized staffing is to implement interdisciplinary teacher teams that have specific team-member responsibilities for the success of each student. During regularly scheduled team planning periods, teachers can identify students who need special attention and follow through by providing extra academic help and coordinating problem-solving approaches with students and their families.

Teams may be especially effective when combined with a teacher-advisory function in which every teacher is assigned a manageable number of students in the school as his or her particular responsibilities for advice and individual support. Evidence from national data on middle schools shows that interdisciplinary teacher teams in departmentalized schools usually contribute to more positive school climates. Qualitative evidence also supports the potential advantages of interdisciplinary teams and adult advisors to provide a more personalized, supportive climate in a departmentalized middle and high school serving at-risk students.

In an age of reform and restructuring, educators are seeking new models to improve their schools. One approach is to replicate the qualities, and hopefully the advantages, of a small school by creating a "school-within-a-school." Separating at-risk students from their more successful counterparts enables both groups to achieve without compromising the needs of either. This approach establishes a smaller educational unit within the school, with a separate educational program, its own staff and students, and its own budget. Several cities, including New York City, Philadelphia, and Chicago, have experimented with this as a method for downsizing.

Education Resource Information Center summarizes existing research on school-within-a-school models and reviews some of the advantages and disadvantages. Large schools have implemented a myriad of programs to downsize or downscale: house plans, mini-schools, learning communities, clusters, charters, and schools-within-schools. Some simply group cohorts of students together while maintaining a symbolic and administrative identification with the larger school. Each model differs from the others on a range of factors including how separate the subunit is from the larger institution and how much autonomy it receives to manage its own education program. The models also differ in terms of programs and organizational structure and practice.

The school-within-a-school model has the greatest levels of autonomy, separateness, and distinctiveness. Students follow a separate education program, have their own faculty, and identify with their subschool unit. Because the school-within-a-school model replicates a small school more closely than the other forms of downsizing, it is most likely to produce the positive effects of small-scale educational organization. At-risk students thrive in self-contained environments.

A review of the literature suggests that implementing the school-within-a-school model has met with varying degrees of success in different settings. The most critical factor for success is a commitment to implementing the program fully, allowing for complete administrative separation of the subschool and the creation of a separate identity. Without full implementation, many of the benefits of small-scale schooling, such as establishing community and symbolic identity, cannot be realized. Staff and student support is also important, and the strengths or weaknesses of a particular plan may vary over the years with personnel changes.

While considerable data exists on outcomes associated with small schools, there is much less evidence about outcomes associated with school-within-a-school programs. In part, this is because very few school-within-a-school models have been fully implemented. A growing body of literature does suggest that downsized school models can have a positive impact on students, including improved attendance rates, improved behavior, greater satisfaction with school, and greater self-esteem. Additionally, there is a positive impact on teachers, who have reported enhanced morale.

Some case studies suggest that a school-within-a-school can contribute to a greater feeling of community among participants, which facilitates student attainment. Research suggests that creating learning communities for young people increased their social commitment to one another and to their teachers, thereby increasing their personal investments in school. Others have identified fiscal and organizational advantages and disadvantages of the school-within-a-school model.

Aside from the advantages of replicating the qualities of a small school, the school-within-a-school appears to be a cost-effective approach to school reform in terms of start-up costs, and in some cases is less expensive to maintain. Among the disadvantages, research suggests this model can sometimes create divisiveness in schools because it tends to realign organizational structures and fracture preexisting relationships.

Conflicts can arise concerning allegiances to the larger school versus the smaller school unit, thus creating rivalries. Other critics maintain that subschool groupings can lead to inequitable tracking if only one population is targeted for a subschool. Another critique argues that the school-within-a-school model may negatively affect school coherence and the role of the principal, two areas of concern in the literature on effective schools.

The school-within-a-school model may be an effective and affordable way to capture the benefits of smaller-scale schooling within larger school buildings to serve at-risk students. While research results are limited, the school-within-a-school model has the potential to contribute to a greater sense of student well-being, a sense of student community, and higher student achievement and educational attainment.

This model seems to hold promise especially for disadvantaged students, who are positively affected by smaller schools but are more likely to attend larger schools. Because a subschool model can be adopted in an existing building structure, it is a cost-effective approach to school reform; however, the challenge lies in successful implementation. Chapter 8 provides insight on best curriculum practices for educating today's at-risk students.

ESSENTIAL IDEAS TO REMEMBER

Many public schools are not designed to ensure the success of students at risk. We must examine the systems in which our districts, schools, and classrooms operate and ask what the systems themselves are doing to educate and transform the lives of at-risk students. There must be a shift to a more equitable system. School leaders know that certain things must be in place for learning to happen, including, but not limited to, varying instructional approaches to match the learning styles of students, differentiating instruction, consistently exposing students to high-quality instruction, and consistently implementing instructional best practices.

All students should feel like they belong in school. Yet, at-risk students believe that the education system does not belong to them, and that they do not belong in it. Changing this perception requires intentional, sustained effort on the part of educators. Expanded school guidance programs are needed to focus on the positive development of student attitudes and habits of mind that lead to success in and out of school.

School leaders must develop policies to guide expectations and provide the resources to support implementation. In response, local districts, schools, and organizations must take thoughtful actions—building on assets and addressing needs appropriate for educating at-risk learners. Creating a school-within-a-school can be a more cost-effective method of school reform than opening an entirely new school. Saving money on start-up and operation costs can mean there is more available to spend on instruction and learning materials. The advantages of a school-within-a-school for students at risk are:

- Many at-risk students attend large or departmentalized schools, where they receive daily instruction from several different teachers. Research indicates students in such schools tend to feel more alienated from their teachers and peers. This feeling of alienation can lead to discipline problems and lower student participation in school activities.
- The potential for stronger relationships between students and teachers. There can be less of a chance that a student will get lost in the crowd or that his or her academic or emotional needs will go unnoticed.
- If students know that someone is counting on them to be at school every day, they may feel more engaged in school and, therefore, more motivated to do well in their classes. Some studies have shown that this type of downsizing can result in better attendance and behavior, as well as improved academic performance. In a smaller environment, a student may also have better opportunities for leadership and recognition.
- It's also possible that a school-within-a-school is providing an educational focus or academic opportunities that are not provided in a traditional school. Students may still have access to common areas and facilities that are intended for everyone on the campus, such as the gym, the playground, the cafeteria, a performing arts space, and the media center. A large building or campus shared by multiple schools is more likely to have these features than a freestanding, small school.

Chapter Eight

Customized Curriculum Strategies

As we continue to delve deeper into best practices to help at-risk students succeed, we can attest that several components are involved: identifying at-risk characteristics, implementing the behavior system, providing appropriate RtI, and adopting a school-within-a school model. How and what at-risk students learn (the curriculum) is the bridge that takes them to the other side, to a place where they are successful rather than failing.

The quality of the relationships amongst at-risk students often factors in the quantity and depth of learning. Effectively reaching at-risk students depends primarily on building strong, positive relationships. Staff must also ensure that their relationships with *all* students are positive and supportive as well. Too often, students feel rejected or isolated when they perceive other students are being treated harshly or unfairly. Remember, one's perception is their reality. Verbal and nonverbal behavior can contribute to the overall tone of the class. In a respectful environment, all students feel valued and safe, which encourages them to take intellectual risks.

Next, students need to adopt a system that fosters success. For example, they should use a daily agenda book for assignments and communication. Agendas are useful for building a positive school routine. Consistency is critical to maintaining academic focus. If necessary, ask teachers to double-check and initial the agenda book to be certain the necessary information is there. In addition to bolstering grades, this daily exercise in organization gives students a sense of control over the academic process and helps build confidence.

Finally, students must find an organizational system that works for them. An agenda book is inconsequential if it's buried under loose papers and books. The best system for students with weak organizational skills is a colored folder system. A red folder for science is easily found in the bottom of a locker. A blue folder can be for their most dreaded class. Make it simple and memorable. Often, a student's entire day is ruined because he or she cannot find an assignment. If the pattern is repeated, students begin to shut down in class, believing that he or she will not pass the class.

Student engagement is the centerpiece for teaching at-risk students. When students are engaged in learning, they are not just busy or always on task. Rather, they are intellectually active in learning the content before them. The critical distinction between a classroom in which students are compliant and busy and one in which they are engaged is that in the latter, students are developing their understanding through what they do. They may be selecting their work from either teacher-arranged or student-driven assignments, and making important contributions to the intellectual climate of the class.

The activities and assignments are the cornerstone of student engagement. Activities and assignments that promote learning require student thinking, emphasize depth over breadth, and may allow students to exercise some choice. The instructional materials used can have an enormous impact on a student's learning experience. Educating at-risk students requires teachers to select materials that are better suited to engaging them in deep, rich learning as well as academic vigor. Materials reflecting students' culture and experiences achieve the best results when used to inspire and to redirect negative habits.

A lesson in which students are engaged usually has a discernible structure: a beginning, a middle, and an end, with scaffolding provided by the teacher or by the activities themselves. Student tasks are organized to provide cognitive challenge, and students are encouraged to reflect on what they have done and what they have learned. That is, there is closure to the lesson, in which students derive important learning from their own actions. This process is referred to as students' self-reflection or self-assessment of what they've learned. This is critical in order for students to take ownership of their learning.

Here is an example of an effective lesson for at-risk students: the social studies assignment required students to make a timeline of the most important years in their lives. An eighth-grade boy proceeded to point out the two most important years in his life. He whispered, "This is the year my father died, and this is the year my mother went to jail." When asked about his current living arrangements, he stated that he lives with his aunt and her five children.

The realization was stark. Whatever is being taught may not be the focus when students are faced with family adversities. Is a quality education important to his future? Yes! Absolutely! Education is more important for this child than those in stable situations. The challenge for those who work with at-risk children is how to make education a focus for them when they are concerned primarily with survival. Whether their at-risk situation is caused by family upheaval, transience, abuse, poverty, or other factors, the challenge for these students is the same.

A set of strategies must be in place so these students can focus more on education and less on personal survival. The middle-school years are critical, often making or breaking students. At-risk issues usually begin in middle school and continue through high school. By planning curriculum specifically for at-risk students, you can improve their chances of academic and social success.

When planning curriculum for at-risk students, teachers should implement a student-centered approach. Tap into the students' past learning experiences in order to expand their understanding of concepts with which they are already familiar—and then go deeper into that familiar topic to show students different levels of analysis. As curriculum is developed throughout the year, it should relate new ideas or information to what students already know and understand to encourage more meaningful learning experiences.

The at-risk learner struggles with connecting traditional learning formats to an authentic learning experience. Understanding by Design (UbD), developed by Grant Wiggins, president of Authentic Education, and Jay McTighe, a notable education leader, is a powerful way of thinking purposefully about curricular planning and school reform, but is not a program or recipe. UbD reflects the convergence of two interdependent ideas: (1) research on learning and cognition that highlights the centrality of teaching and assessing for understanding and (2) a helpful and time-honored process for curriculum writing.

The end goal of UbD is understanding and the ability to transfer learning, connect, comprehend, and use discrete knowledge and skills in context. Evidence of understanding is revealed through performance. When learners transfer knowledge and skills effectively, it is demonstrated by using one or more skills of the six facets of understanding: explain, interpret, apply, shift perspective, empathize, and self-assess.

Planning is best done backward from the desired results and the transfer tasks that embody the goals. The backward design approach is developed in three stages:

Stage 1: Identify desired results: What should students be able to do with their learning?

- Transfer goals
- Essential questions and understandings
- Knowledge and skill objectives
- Relevant standards and other established goals

Stage 2: Determine acceptable evidence: What is valid evidence of their ability to meet the long-term transfer goal?

- Performance tasks
- Evaluative criteria

Stage 3: Plan learning experiences and instruction: What learning experiences and instruction do students need to get there?

- An outline of the Learning Plan emphasizing meaning, making, and transfer

UbD transforms standards and other goals into focused learning targets based on transfer tasks and "big ideas." Big ideas require "unpacking" (using only what you need to reach the goal), provide lasting value beyond the classroom, and are measurable. The learning environment should have high expectations and incentives for students to come to understand the big ideas and answer the essential questions. UbD reflects a continuous improvement approach from the design to the learning. The assessment results, the quality of student work, and the degree of learner engagement determines the next instructional direction.

Teaching for understanding is the central premise of UbD. It should be evident in course design, teacher and student attitudes, and the classroom learning environment. There should be a coherent curriculum design and clear distinctions between big ideas and essential questions. Teachers should tell students about big ideas and essential questions, performance requirements, and evaluative criteria at the beginning of the unit or lesson. Big ideas are worth exploring and understanding in depth. And essential questions are designed to provoke genuine inquiry and to encourage transfer.

UbD is a perfect learning curriculum model for at-risk students because they often live with the end in mind. They frequently make decisions on predictions. For example, truant students stop attending school because they predict they will flunk out due to lack of credits or failing grades. Effective UbD units or lessons for at-risk students would use positive outcomes (stage 1), realistic evidence of students' determination (stage 2), and the beginning steps needed to succeed (stage 3).

In addition to enhancing the learning experience through UbD, supplemental materials that target specific at-risk characteristics and behaviors should also be included in the curriculum. For example, students who are affiliated with or curious about gangs could benefit from education on the origin and evolution of gangs. Homelessness, abandonment, and long-term illnesses are adversities that will negatively affect anyone. Students at-risk are slow to recover from adversities because of limited resources. Providing

Stage 1	Stage 2	Stage 3
If the desired end result is for at-risk students to... →	then you need evidence of the students' determination to...→	then the events need to...
Attend school daily with a renewed commitment to learn and achieve.	Adopt the strategies that reduce the influences or triggers that result in non attendance issues.	Help truant students to identify the characteristics that result in truancy and participate in attendance and other programs outlined in their Individual Service Plan (ISP).

Figure 8.1.   The Logic of Backward Design

them with relevant, researched strategies on ways to overcome the specific adversity is a learning bonus.

Grouping students is considered a best practice; but I do not recommend grouping practices used in traditional classrooms for at-risk students. For example, putting gang members at a table to discuss the origin of gangs might not result in a positive learning experience. But when students research their own issue(s), form mixed groups, participate in rich discussions, and complete a group project, the skills used and the knowledge gained helps them to understand how they got where they are and learn what they need to do to reverse the path.

One example of such a project is capstone. A capstone project is usually an undergraduate degree requirement but can easily be adapted for the purpose of educating at-risk students. The project represents work of a more in-depth understanding than what is normally expected and provides an opportunity for students to draw on their methodological, analytical, and substantive learning in a comprehensive manner. For example, a gang member researches the origin and intent of gangs; another student researches the pitfalls of substance abuse; another, abandonment. After in-depth research on a selected topic, the group needs a gatekeeper and a timekeeper.

Model and practice the roles of gatekeeper and a timekeeper. The more time spent in this phase, the better the group experience. Once procedures are established, rich and meaningful discussions evolve. The power behind the discussions is that students have a voice and they are being heard! This becomes an "ah-ha" moment for many at-risk students; the win, lose, or draw in teaching and learning. At this juncture, you must know your options: to proceed to the next step of the capstone, go back a step and revise, or start over completely.

Assuming you're ready to proceed, you will want students to produce a visual culminating artifact, for example, a poster board demonstrating the results of the group's research. Art, music, videos, and expert speakers further enhance the learning experience and is highly encouraged when possible. Upon completion, provide an opportunity for your students to showcase their knowledge and understanding through a home-school-community event! Remember, seize any opportunity to encourage and support at-risk students to replace a deficit with an achievement.

In addition to the curriculum models previously highlighted, new technologies can provide meaningful learning experiences for all children—especially those at risk of educational failure. Schools that capitalize on the relationship between technology and education reform will help students to develop higher-order thinking skills and to function effectively in the world beyond the classroom. Achieving such fundamental change requires teachers to transform their basic assumptions about teaching and learning and the kinds of technology applications available for classrooms serving at-risk students.

The vision of classrooms structured around students involved in challenging, long-term projects and focused on meaningful, engaged learning is achievable with hard work and determination. Narrow curricula, rigid instructional strategies, tracking, and pull-out programs hinder the academic achievement of at-risk students. Recent findings indicate that by failure to challenge at-risk students and encouraging them to use complex thinking skills, schools underestimate students' capabilities, postpones interesting work that they could be doing, and deprives them of a meaningful context for learning and mastering the skills that are taught.

In the new vision of challenging learning activities, the curriculum for all students would emphasize the integration of higher-order thinking skills, authentic tasks, and mixed-ability groupings. Instead of students practicing discrete, isolated skills, such as spelling and punctuation done on worksheets, the curriculum would stress composition, comprehension, and applications of skills. Rather than treating basic skills as an obstacle, schools would give at-risk students opportunities to learn and practice basic skills in the context of working on authentic tasks.

At-risk students should be in more heterogeneous groupings as part of collaborative classrooms and less in ability groupings or pull-out classes for compensatory instruction. They should be judged on their ability to perform a complex task and to reflect on and describe the thinking that went into it rather than on their facility with multiple-choice tests. An emerging body of research suggests that when technology is used in classrooms, fulfilling such a vision can be especially advantageous to at-risk children. Technology can engage students in challenging, authentic learning.

Teachers can draw on technology applications to simulate real-world activities and create actual environments for experimentation, so that students can carry out authentic tasks as real workers would, explore new terrains, meet people of different cultures, and use a variety of tools to gather information and solve problems. Research on classrooms that have put constructivist teaching and learning models into practice also indicates that technology can enhance student engagement and productivity.

More specifically, technology increases the complexity of the tasks that students can perform successfully, raises student motivation, and leads to changes in classroom roles and organization. These role changes—with students moving toward more self-reliance and peer coaching, and teachers functioning more as facilitators than as lecturers—support educational reform goals for all students.

Technology also can help students develop positive cooperative-learning relationships, enabling them to work together while researching topics and creating presentations. In such relationships, students help each other learn. Students with special needs may require more coaching in computer-based activities, but they will benefit from the experience of learning with and from other students.

Traditionally, schools have not focused on technology as a means to support engaged learning. When computers are present in schools serving at-risk students, they usually are used for drill-and-practice programs on basic skills rather than as tools to support students in designing their own projects. Schools typically promote learning with technology through the use of stand-alone devices or environments.

Today, educational researchers are calling for very different uses of technology. They promote classroom learning activities in which students work in small groups rather than in isolation or as a whole class. The technologies used in the classroom are not those designed explicitly to teach basic skills, but rather are real-world applications that support research, design, analysis, composition, and communication.

Technology has tremendous power to help students obtain, organize, manipulate, and display information. Students can use technology tools, such as word processing, database, design, and graphing software, in the same ways as professionals in business, communications, and research. Such practical uses of technology contrast sharply with the more didactic technology applications designed explicitly for instruction.

Using technology for meaningful activities also helps integrate a variety of disciplines, more closely resembling activities that people undertake in the world beyond the classroom. For example, word processing is real-world technology that can help students develop writing and thinking skills. Using the computer, students write longer, more complex sentences and are more willing to revise and edit their work. They are able to concentrate on the thoughts they want to express rather than the mechanical skills of penman-ship, spelling, and grammar.

Many changes will be necessary if schools are to provide such exciting, technology-supported activities for all students. Time, effort, and resources are needed to bring students to a level of computer literacy. At-risk children from low-income families are less likely to have access to computers in their homes and often attend schools with less computer equipment. After technol-ogies are obtained, school districts need to ensure that all students have technological equity and equal access to the learning tools of the twenty-first century.

Furthermore, technology-based instruction provides built-in support for struggling learners. A crucial web-based design consideration for at-risk learners is the provision of enriched curriculum that is scaffolded, offers ample explanations and corrective practice, and has a variety of tools to construct their work. However, technology-based learning may not be appli-cable to all learners. Technology is an effective resource, but some consider-ation must be made before implementing it. Teachers must be open to the possibility that learners may need a different venue for their education and be prepared to offer that, as in traditional differentiated instruction.

Obtaining the technology for schools serving at-risk students is just the tip of the iceberg. Because students often receive computer-based instruction in a separate computer lab, regular classroom teachers may have little contact with the technology. Teachers need support not just for learning to use new technologies but also for acquiring skills in designing and implementing high-quality, student-centered projects. Teachers also need a strong system of professional development and ongoing support if they are to achieve the dramatic changes in teaching approaches called for by technology implemen-tation.

In order to promote engaged learning through technology for at-risk stu-dents, teachers must:

- Ensure that the classroom reflects a collaborative atmosphere as a prelude to implementing technology-supported projects.
- Develop classroom activities incorporating challenging, authentic tasks with technology tools used as supports when they add significant value. Seek opportunities to collaborate with other teachers and work in teams to design and implement technology-supported projects.
- Become comfortable learning about technology along with students, and repeatedly model higher-order thinking skills so that students can see positive ways to approach new learning challenges.
- Promote cooperative learning in the classroom so that students work to-gether and learn from each other.

- Design activities so that every student has something to offer. Students who previously have had little success in learning activities may feel very successful in a technology-rich classroom that emphasizes meaningful, authentic tasks.
- Develop procedures and checklists to help monitor and document each student's progress.

Through the curriculum practice of UbD, capstone projects, and effective use of technology, at-risk students become equipped with a solid educational platform. They will start to recognize the context connections in learning and transfer them to real-world experiences that will ultimately lead them to the personal transformation necessary in order to become successful. Educators must shift from teaching subjects to educating students. Relating education to careers further helps at-risk students to make meaningful and lasting connections.

Yesterday's educational system is inadequate to meet today's realities. According to Gates Foundation, nearly 47 percent of high-school dropouts said a major reason for dropping out was that classes were not interesting. Many at-risk students do poorly in school for just that reason. For others, if not most, conventional schoolwork has little to do with what goes on outside the classroom. With a clearer understanding of the foundations causing at-risk behaviors, schools can no longer teach in isolation. We must connect what our students learn to what they can do.

School-to-Work is a partnership between employers and schools to provide opportunities for students to learn about the world of work. For some students, exposure to the workplace enables them to explore career ideas. For others, it's a chance to think strategically about college. Learning becomes more relevant and engaging than in a traditional classroom setting. School-to-Work programs can help prepare young people to be successful in life by building such skills as how to make decisions, solve problems, work with others, and bring about positive change.

Being able to participate in the workforce is part of becoming a productive citizen. Also, preparing at-risk students for occupations may reduce social problems, such as drug abuse, teen pregnancy, and crime because they begin to cultivate attention in other aspects of life. Real education is not just the academics or acquiring knowledge but also the application of that knowledge, which is the gist of relating school to work. With the integration of school and work-based learning, students are able to see how what they learn in school connects to the workplace.

For many at-risk students, applied learning may be the only avenue that works for them and applying knowledge on the job could provide the hook to interest them in a whole range of course material and activities that they otherwise would not have learned. Furthermore, the very nature of School-to-

Work activities—contextual, hands-on, and offering more choice—can meet the learning needs of students and increase their engagement in the learning process. A critical element of fostering learning is to have students carry out tasks and solve problems in an environment that reflects the multiple uses to which their knowledge will be used in the future.

Preparing at-risk students for a School-to-Work mindset can be challenging and may prove difficult without successfully implementing all of the strategies that were previously discussed. The journey may be long and the road rocky. Setbacks and delays are often a part of any transformation, especially when coaching at-risk students to replace destructive habits with productive ones. Once students accept the challenge to move from limited learning to an active participant in their transformation, success is reachable.

Education with a purpose occurs when relevant, challenging learning environments are implemented and maintained by partnerships between educators, community leaders, and employers. The magic happens when educators take responsibility for providing academic vigor, community leaders establish the school/business partnerships, and employers create the pathway for at-risk students to make the connection between school and work.

It is hard to imagine what type of skills will be needed in the years to come. But we know that employers look for employees who possess skills capable of managing projects, providing leadership to multifunctional teams, anticipating opportunities or problems and researching and pulling together subject matter experts to take advantage of new ideas. Employers look to hire young men and women to compete for STEM (science, technology, engineering and mathematics) careers.

Smart businesses invest in education by partnering with schools to provide the bridge from learning to working. Through a meaningful and educational engagement with students, they develop a talent pipeline of students who are ready for college or careers. Communities who fail to partner with educational institutions may lose revenue, resulting in businesses closing, thereby contributing to the cycle of poverty.

Another bonus for businesses to partner with educators is to prepare at-risk students with twenty-first-century workplace skills. At-risk students need to be encouraged to practice higher-order thinking and leadership skills, such as problem-solving, synthesizing data, and processing information from multiple sources. They also need to know how to function as a part of a cross-functional team. Thankfully, more and more business leaders are coming to understand the direct linkage between workforce and economic development in education. However, there is still plenty of work to be done.

Businesses pay the price when they spend resources to recruit and hire students only to find out that they do not have the twenty-first-century skills necessary to succeed in the workplace today.

And they pay the price when they have to send students back to school to acquire these critical workplace skills necessary to succeed. Taxpayers pay the price when students are unprepared to take care of themselves and their future families.

As businesses begin to grapple with looming skills shortages, it makes sense for them to be supportive of high schools in general and specifically career-oriented curriculum that provides direct links to the workplace. Unfortunately, it doesn't happen without a vision and a plan. Despite the efforts of countless dedicated teachers and administrators—not to mention billions of dollars spent on education reform—public education continues to fall short of its potential. With this in mind, it is critical that schools build and foster partnerships that prepare at-risk students for career options. An ideal school/business partnership provides:

- alignment and articulation with school curriculum
- industry-recognized skills and knowledge
- opportunities for job-shadowing, site visits, internships, and other work-site learning experiences
- resources ranging from mentoring to funding

The benefits of a successful school/business partnership are:

- improved grades and attendance
- more at-risk students graduate from high school
- at-risk students earn higher scores on standardized academic, career, and technical tests
- enrollments in postsecondary programs increase
- high-school students demonstrate better preparedness to make informed career choices

The fact that School-to-Work programs may help students to see the relevance of school to the world of work means that these students will see the connection between acquiring higher skills to obtain the higher-wage jobs. Students thus have an economic incentive to do well in school. Providing students with a set of job-ready skills and the motivation to continuously upgrade their skills will translate into shorter unemployment spells, shorter welfare rolls, and produce citizens who contribute to society.

ESSENTIAL IDEAS TO REMEMBER

At-risk children in this country are still denied the education they need to find meaningful and well-paying jobs. Today we all pay a price when employers cannot expand because they cannot find the skilled, educated employees they need. If we continue to undereducate students in our country, we will pay the price for many decades to come. Our economy urgently needs more young people with skills in science and mathematics and with the ability to think critically and work collaboratively.

With emphasis on college-readiness for elementary grades, at-risk students need a better support system to encourage those dreams. They also need to be connected with peers who want to pursue college, with young adults who have just completed college, and be able to connect the learning to career choices. Many students who enter college are unprepared academically for college-level work.

School-to-work programs provide more training so employers can do a better job of connecting with learners, and teachers can use different styles of teaching to engage students and deliver content in a manner that will resonate and inspire. Businesses should establish collaborations between higher education and school districts to cocreate and codeliver preservice and inservice programs with an emphasis on school climate, engaging diverse classrooms, and instructional strategies for at-risk students.

We need our youth to become leaders, problem-solvers, skilled craftspeople, technicians, researchers, educators, and health-care professionals. For our economy to recover and progress, we need every young mind prepared to compete and win in a high-tech, fast-changing global economy. If we fail to develop our most precious resource—the talent and imagination of every young person—we have little hope for our future prosperity.

Increasing academic success is about relationships, relevance, and rigor. What at-risk students need is exactly what all students need. They need teachers and school leaders who have high expectations of them. They need rigorous and relevant curriculum that engages, challenges, and connects them from the world they know to the world they need to know. They need more academic supports that would help them succeed. They need teachers and school leaders with the skills to connect with them and teach them well.

Effective use of technology is critical when working with at-risk students. When students are using technology as a tool or a support for communicating with others, they are in an active role rather than the passive role of recipient of information transmitted by a teacher, textbook, or broadcast. The student is actively making choices about how to generate, obtain, manipulate, or display information. Technology use allows many more students to be actively thinking about information, making choices, and executing skills than is typical in teacher-led lessons.

The way students learn is fundamentally changing. A flexible, blended classroom model is replacing the one-size-fits-all classroom approach that was confined to set hours and locations. Teachers are using digital technologies to engage students with more personalized learning experiences. Students are collaborating across geographical boundaries, and consuming and producing innovative education-related content. Some of the benefits of technology use in the classroom are:

- Increased motivation and self esteem
- Accomplishment of more complex tasks
- More collaboration with peers
- Increased use of outside resources

A progressive curriculum is critical to student success. Consistent exposure to effective learning opportunities can overcome obstacles to learning. In addition, high expectations and a cultural competence among teachers, school staff, administrators, curriculum, and assessment promote academic success and less remediation. All students need a well-taught, rigorous, world-class curriculum that prepares them for success in school and beyond.

Chapter Nine

Breaking the Barriers

The litany of barriers to promote effective school reform for at-risk students usually stems from insufficient or unavailable resources. All too often, at-risk students bring a variety of problems to school such as low academic achievement, family adversities, poverty, untreated mental health issues, and more. Effective school–home–community partnerships have the potential to expand opportunities for improving the quality of life for at-risk students by acknowledging that barriers exist. Schools have long understood that if they are to meet the needs of at-risk students, the barriers that impede their success must be effectively addressed.

A comprehensive behavior system is fundamental in order to expand support for educating at-risk students. Effective partnerships require an infrastructure of organizational and operational pieces in order to provide oversight, leadership, resources, and ongoing support for implementing programs that serve at-risk students. These tasks require educators at various levels to commit their time and resources in order to fully enhance parental and community involvement. When time is insufficient and resources are limited, implementation barriers to school reform are born.

This leadership team should consist of a teacher, social worker, psychologist, RtI coach, nurse, principal, and community representatives from both business and church. Coordinating these entities can be overwhelming for the members who provide direct services; therefore, schools may turn to site-based assistance. As a result, reform may be implemented in fragmentation. Matters related to school–home–community partnerships appear regularly on school board agendas, but are often handled in an ad hoc manner, without appropriate attention to the whole picture, resulting in unconnected support services needed to combat at-risk behaviors.

The barriers to implementing a comprehensive continuum of interventions need to be understood in order to be addressed. And addressing these challenges requires reframing the roles of professionals who work in schools and neighboring communities. Their new roles entail multifaceted functions, providing vision and leadership that transforms how schools and communities address each barrier and train staff on best practices. Next, we'll explore five common barriers and solutions to implementing a comprehensive behavior system designed to educate and transform the lives of at-risk students.

SCHOOL DISTRICTS ALLOW BUDGETARY CONCERNS TO LIMIT THEIR FOCUS ON ADDRESSING SCHOOL VIOLENCE

School violence needs no introduction and has created so much panic among parents, that many are afraid to send their children to school. School violence is a major concern for educators as well. The distress of potential violence in school weighs heavily on the minds and hearts of educators working with at-risk students. All of the at-risk characteristics previously identified can become triggers for youth to engage in school violence. Although nothing specific can predict the violent attitude of the students, schools must implement strategies that determine and gauge their propensity for violence.

Many school districts remain unprepared to address school violence. For example, after a student has committed a violent or criminal act, he or she is subject to a suspension, expulsion, or alternative placement. School violence statistics have proven that those measures are inadequate because they are reactive rather than preventive. Unfortunately, district budgets usually dictate the degree of safety schools receive. This *must* change if the goal is to prevent school violence.

Solution: School districts must proactively address violence in schools. Large school districts may look to reduce costs by implementing practices such as locker searches, drug-sniffing dogs, and closed-lunch campuses. Zero-tolerance assemblies and violence-prevention programs may encourage awareness in students and staff, but without long-term effect. Students prone to violence are not impacted by "just say no." While these strategies are certainly helpful, they fail to provide an adequate deterrent from potential acts of violence.

Metal detectors, police presence, and appropriately placed security cameras provide maximum measures to protect students and staff against school violence, but at a significant cost to school districts. Aren't saving lives worth the cost? State-of-the-art technology, the best administrators and teachers, and the most celebrated curriculum means little when lives are in jeopardy every day. With strategic implementation planning, schools can be prepared to combat school violence.

Cost-free strategies that help prevent school violence can be in place while the more costly prevention plans are being implemented. The first strategy is to put measures in place to identify and address bullying. Bullying is a major factor in school violence and adequate attention and care should be given to treat this malice. Students who bully usually display aggressive behavior that involves a real or perceived power imbalance. The behavior is repeated, or has the potential to be repeated, over time. Bullying includes actions such as making threats, spreading rumors, attacking someone physically or verbally, and intentionally excluding someone from a group.

Second, districts are advised to incorporate Transcendental Meditation (TM), an effortless procedure practiced twenty minutes each day while sitting comfortably with the eyes closed. It's the most widely practiced, most researched, and most effective method of self-development. Meditation practices are a benefit for *all* students, but especially for those at risk. School violence rarely erupts without careful plotting on the part of the offender(s). Imagine how the practice of TM might have altered that infamous day at Columbine High. Could something as simple as having students close their eyes and sit in stillness for twenty minutes a day help address school violence?

According to the National Center for Biotechnology, research suggests that the chronic stress and psychological trauma associated with persistent exposure to community violence causes the body to produce toxic levels of stress hormones that increase health risk and inhibit cognitive function. Meditation also helps improve mental health and stability as well as promotes relaxation without medication. TM is not a religion, a philosophy, or a way of life, but simply a technique that helps people to calm their bodies and minds. Over time, TM can help a student prone to violence to replace violent tendencies with calm and rational behavior choices.

In a controlled study, a group of urban high-school students were assigned to TM, fifteen minutes at school and fifteen minutes at home every day, while the control group received fifteen minutes of daily health education. After four months, the meditation group missed significantly less school and had fewer infractions and behavior-related suspensions than the control group. Schools in Detroit, San Francisco, Connecticut, and Arizona have already integrated TM into the school day. While research on the benefits of TM still has a ways to go, schools could be proactive and provide students with education on how they can manage the stresses in their lives.

If schools learn that a student or group may act violently in future, they can immediately invoke SAS to help prevent possible acts of violence. In doing so, it is important that each SAS team member is trained to deal with a potentially violent student. When talking to a violent or potentially violent student, respect his or her silence and let the student talk when he or she needs to talk. Some other tips are:

- Find what is considered a "safe zone" within the school and always have others present when speaking to the student.
- Avoid language that may tease or shame the student because he or she may retaliate if feeling threatened or diminished.
- Respond with short statements rather than long ones, because this is the student's time to talk.

EDUCATORS WORKING WITH AT-RISK STUDENTS FAIL TO DEVELOP A SUCCINCT VISION, CORE VALUES, AND MISSION STATEMENTS

Another barrier to successful school reform for at-risk students is the absence of a shared vision, core values, and mission statements. In the case of a school-within-a-school model, the at-risk "wing" should have separate statements from the rest of the school. Students at risk and the team who works with them have different values and require different measures of growth, accomplishment, and self-reflection.

Vision, values, and mission statements should drive the decisions made to improve teaching and learning. Not everyone understands how to develop these statements. As a result, school policies and procedures are often misaligned. To further complicate matters, schools may begin to adopt practices stemming from inconsistent statements that contradict the school's culture. So how can we hold students, parents, and community accountable if we convey inconsistent messages?

Solution: School-within-a-school models or residential placement facilities designed to rehabilitate at-risk students need an attainable vision, core values, and mission statements. Core values are traits or qualities that represent the highest priorities, deeply-held beliefs, and fundamental driving forces. They are made accessible by translating them into value statements that define desires or describe actions that are the fundamental core values held by everyone. The vision statement and core values are instrumental in developing a mission statement. The vision statement relates to the end goal and the mission statement reflects how that goal will be reached.

Vision Statement: [Name of school/program] is a learning environment that challenges students to reach their academic, civic, and social potential in a diverse community so that they may become productive members within their communities.

Core Values: The acronym *C.A.R.E.S.* is a tool for remembering and expressing the values. In the final document, each word is defined by a series of value statements that describe how the value is expressed.

- Compassion
- Accountability
- Responsibility
- Empowerment
- Sincerity

Mission Statement: Through the daily decision to practice C.A.R.E.S., [Name of school/program] will promote making healthy lifestyle choices that transform the lives of each student.

EDUCATORS AND COMMUNITY MEMBERS FAIL TO COLLABORATE IN IMPLEMENTING PROGRAMS DESIGNED TO HELP AT-RISK STUDENTS BECOME SUCCESSFUL

Educators need to specify the problems. One of the greatest barriers to improving educational opportunities for students at risk is the practice of minimizing the various problems they bear. Regardless of justification, this lack of specificity leads to an endless searching for something or someone to blame. Parents blame schools; teachers blame parents and administrators; administrators blame teachers or unions. Generic blaming of others only continues the current gridlock and perpetuates the current problems. For example, if dropout prevention is a goal, then districts should look at implementing a credit-recovery program.

Next, schools need SAS partnerships. At-risk students experience a variety of complex problems that require comprehensive interventions. Establishing a continuum of services can be challenging without sufficient funding and resources. Also, given the likelihood that most of the problems are chronic and multifaceted, support is needed to address root causes, thereby minimizing the need for separate programs for each issue. The support needed may involve horizontal and vertical restructuring of programs and services, which may be difficult at the school or district levels alone.

Student and family assistance is the area where most SAS services are concentrated. Social, physical, and mental health support should be available in an integrated system to reduce chaotic classrooms. Without SAS linkages, teachers' effectiveness in accommodating a variety of issues decreases. Classroom instruction, statewide initiatives, special-education needs, and professional development also suffer in the absence of comprehensive support systems. Sadly, this is frequently the stage at which most at-risk students drop out of school.

At-risk students and their families are regularly confronted with a variety of transitions such as changing homes, transferring schools, placement change from traditional to alternative school, and reshuffling of teachers. SAS provides communication strategies to aide in these transitions and ensures that ongoing supports continue in the next phase of intervention. Without appropriate transitional support, at-risk students may fall through the cracks and the previous hurdles that were gained may be lost.

Marginal implementation and unconnected services can be the difference between life and death. Factors to prevent school violence, child abuse, and suicide are severely hindered without a SAS support linkage. Schools need to respond to a crisis quickly and competently in order to minimize its impact and duration. A crisis team trained in emergency response should be in place at all times. Effective crisis management requires systematic programs for district-wide emergency response efforts. This cannot be accomplished when programs and services work independently of each other.

In addition, educators need to understand the demands and limitations of programs. Even a program independently validated and compatible with local predilections has limitations that must be addressed. For example, school-to-work programs can be particularly difficult to set up and institutionalize because they require significant employer participation. Businesses may shun participation because of the cost and time constraints. The costs include expenses for the development and administration of the program, the supervisor's, mentor's, or intern's salaries, and miscellaneous costs such as equipment, uniforms, and other related tools.

One area where the lack of participation is evident in school-to-work programs is job shadowing. Job shadowing allows students to follow an individual for a day, to get a snapshot in the career choice that they are interested in. Unfortunately, it is hard for the employer and employee to commit to job shadowing because they may lose productivity, which results in loss of revenue for that day. A useful alternative for a business is an internship, which allows smaller segments of students to work at the business. This allows the student to understanding of the position and allows the business time to attend to their work instead of focusing on the student.

Internships, however, can cause problems for the business because, many times, they are paid positions. Internships can be accomplished in two different ways. A long-term internship is normally four to six weeks and involves twenty-plus hours per week. This is normally a paid internship. A short-term internship is considered anything less than four weeks and without pay. Also, training is required for each intern. If the student chooses not to stay with the business after his or her internship is complete, the business loses the money that was invested in the student without receiving the benefits of the student's training.

Job shadowing and internships are time consuming for both the school and the business. The process to set up an internship or job shadowing date that will work for the student and the business can be challenging. Some businesses select students through a hiring process. This includes a basic application, group interview, attendance and discipline records, and letters of recommendation. Training the individual in the skill area can be costly, too. Some businesses prefer students to already know how to complete different aspects that are required for the position. These businesses may not have resources to train students in all areas of the position.

Employee retention is another problem in most businesses without adding school-to-work programs. Businesses are finding a greater loss in retention even after taking the time and providing the resources for the students to learn the skill. Students in paid positions arranged as part of school-to-work programs are employed in a wider array of industries and receive more training than other students in unpaid positions. It is from this additional training that the students are going to different positions and leaving the businesses that have invested so much in them.

Finally, some businesses just do not want to hire *any* high-school students, especially those at risk because of their poor attendance, disruptive behavior, and limited skills. Employers express dissatisfaction with the job that high schools are doing to prepare their graduates for several workforce skills because of the graduates' inability to read and understand basic directives, to think analytically, and to apply what they learn in school to solve real-world problems.

Solution: Many at-risk students are in danger of failing in their current grade or of dropping out of school entirely. Traditional methods are often inadequate for providing support to at-risk students, either because the students are not present to receive it or their problems are multi-faceted and require intensive intervention(s). There are a number of interventions that can be implemented for supporting at-risk students, some with policy changes, but many without.

Implement Credit-Recovery Programs

Educators today are finding that online and blended learning are effective ways to reach students who fail one or more courses before they become disengaged, or who seek an alternative education program. As online learning moves past the early-adopter phase, the growth of online programs focused on credit recovery has redefined how educational technology can be used to address the needs of at-risk students. Credit recovery refers to a student passing, and receiving credit for, a course that the student previously

attempted but was unsuccessful in earning academic credit toward graduation.

Credit-recovery programs can be an important strategy for dropout prevention. In these programs, students can work closely with teachers either
individually or in small groups to complete coursework or credits required to
graduate. In other words, credit-recovery programs need to address the challenges that prevented students from previous success. This may include flexible pacing and schedules of instruction, adapting instructional methods and
content to students' skill levels and learning styles, extra practice and fre-
quent assessments to inform instruction and to provide feedback to students.

At-risk students should be able to earn credit for learning life skills that
help them to get back on track. Accreditation conflicts can be addressed
through committee research of state law and committee consensus. This opportunity is a small investment on the part of a school district but could have
a huge payoff for the student. Credit-recovery opportunities for students who
have significant issues can be the difference between a high-school dropout
and a high-school graduate.

Create Student Advocacy Support Partnerships

SAS is designed to provide students with a comprehensive management care
plan of services. Neighboring communities often have common concerns and
may have programs that can share resources. One way to reduce costs is for
communities to pool resources by forming a "School Community Council."
School Community Councils are forums for exchanging ideas about how to
improve student achievement among the school's stakeholders: principals,
teachers, school staff, parents, students, and community members.

School Community Councils are a major part of the overall leadership
structure. They are a group of people who are elected by their peers to advise
the principal on specific matters that affect student achievement and school
improvement. Their primary role is to participate in the process that ensures
that the needs of all students are specifically addressed in the overall education plan for the school. They prepare an Academic and Financial Plan, a
document that highlights the goals for the school, the programs, and the
available resources to reach these goals.

School Community Councils are forums for open discussion and problem-solving related to student achievement. Recent research suggests that
when done well, this process contributes to improved school culture and a
strong professional community of educators. In addition, effective decision-
making supports improved classroom practice and student learning. These
results indicate that democratic structures like School Community Councils
are integral to school and student success. They are useful for linking schools

and community resources and integrating the efforts of high schools and their feeder middle and elementary schools.

School Community Councils coordinate and integrate programs serving a district's pre-K through high school(s) in its community as well as provide educators with formative and summative assessments on the interventions in place. At-risk students benefit from this type of linkage because (1) support relationships have been established, (2) the continuum of support remains intact, and (3) monitoring and tweaking interventions can be performed expeditiously.

Effective school councils should identify a "point person" who has the most positive rapport with an at-risk student, and let that person know immediately of the challenges facing the child. Ask this educator for help in working through any rough spots. If one teacher on the team is sold on this student's potential, he or she can spread the word to the entire team and suggest de-escalating strategies when the student is having a tough day.

Most schools are able to reach at-risk students when they are an integral part of the community. For schools to be integral, steps must be taken to create and maintain collaborative connections. For example, schools need to connect to public and private agencies, higher education, businesses, and churches. Such collaboration increases achievement because at-risk students need to receive the same message from multiple sources of information, which helps reduce poor behavior choices and addresses the triggers. To begin the process, create an action plan with a timeline to accomplish the tasks below:

- Appoint principals who have a proven track record of working with at-risk students.
- Select teachers carefully. Subject matter expertise and pedagogical skills are a bonus, but if you have to choose, select teachers committed to serving at-risk students first.
- Provide ongoing professional development as a Professional Learning Community (PLC). Don't expect teachers to know how to work together as a cohesive team. Without sufficient support, staff may feel threatened when their routines are questioned.
- To become an effective PLC, the team needs time, resources, and encouragement.
- Enhance developmental literacy. Ensure that every member of the team understands what it means to provide developmentally appropriate education (cognitively, emotionally, physically, and morally) for the youth.
- Know and respect students. To do so, provide individual adult contact and get to know their families. Accept that today's breakthrough may be short-lived. Setbacks are normal with at-risk students.

- Create an atmosphere for success. Establish an environment that provides safety, order, and consistency.
- Demand community support. Insist on adequate support for the at-risk students for the same or fewer dollars as the more socially adjusted.
- Champion your school. To increase the support for and resources of your school, promote it within your community.
- Keep experimenting. Utilize multiple forms of assessment, such as observation, surveys, standardize tests, and external evaluations. Tweak your plan based on your data.
- Don't assume responsibility for all successes or failures. Have the PLC team analyze data, generate alternative solutions, and analyze consequences. Every available person should work for the success of the whole team and the future of the at-risk student in the middle.

Adopt a School-to-Work Program

School-to-work programs are designed to create and support regional, sector-based partnerships among businesses, educational agencies, and workforce organizations. An effective partnership:

- Works with employers to expand opportunities for educational advising services and to integrate work and education.
- Adopts policies that facilitate the transfer of students and educational credit (i.e., articulation) between community colleges and other workforce education providers.
- Streamlines curricula development and approval processes for postsecondary education and training to keep programs current with business needs.
- Embeds support for and bridge programs into relevant workforce development, human services, and career and technical education programs.
- Ensures that employer-focused training programs have strong connections to state and local basic skills and postsecondary programs.
- Develops or improves standards for assessing whether prior on-the-job learning, certifications, and competencies count toward college credit, to promote attainment of postsecondary credentials.

IN AN EFFORT TO IMPROVE ON A BUDGET, SCHOOLS SOMETIMES ADOPT PROGRAMS OR PRACTICES WITHOUT PROVIDING THE NECESSARY RESOURCES

Researchers have argued that technology has the potential to dramatically change the way in which our schools are structured, creating pressure to do away with the division of instructional time into small blocks and discrete disciplines and to rethink the way we use physical classrooms and teaching resources. This practice has resulted in some schools deciding to use technology in order to support changes in school structure but do so without the ongoing professional development that is needed.

Failure to provide adequate professional development in technology presents a myriad of obstacles. Teachers need to be trained in how to use the technology and to apply it instructionally within their domain. Too often, technology training is discontinued after the teachers acquire rudimentary computer literacy or are taught the basics of using a specific piece of software. But it is one thing to be able to open up a piece of spreadsheet software, for example, and quite another to have a repertoire of instructionally useful activities for students to learn mathematical concepts through constructing spreadsheets and graphing the data.

Besides professional development, teachers need adequate time to experiment with technology and to design and implement good technology-based activities. Teachers who frequently use technology agree that such activities not only take longer to implement with students but also require more advance planning and preparation on the teacher's part. Schools that give teachers adequate time to acquire technology skills, plan technology-based activities, and share their technology-related work with each other are more successful in improving learning opportunities for at-risk students.

Another obstacle is that many low-SES households may not have technology for educational purposes, yet school curriculum requires technology-supported assignments. So when technology is used for group work, teachers need to be particularly vigilant that those students with access to technology at home do not take over the tasks of the entire group. Teachers need to teach students how to share technology leadership. They must ensure that all students have an opportunity to participate in the technology activity and to gain the essential skills and knowledge that the activity is designed to teach.

A major challenge facing teachers is maintaining the focus on strong instructional content. Teachers and students may become mesmerized by the glamorous features of the ever-evolving technology and may fail to fully grasp the content. To avoid this situation, teachers must discipline themselves to design or select technology-based activities that have specific learning goals along with activities that are fun and interesting. In some cases, teachers may want to disable some of the options open to students in order to help them focus on the essential features.

In addition, some educators and parents are skeptical of technology approaches to teaching and learning for at-risk students. They fear that the students will fail to acquire the fundamental proficiencies needed for further education. Many schools using technology with low-SES students prefer to focus on technology applications that have been proven to increase basic skills. Some educators note that although drill-and-practice software does not prepare students for tasks in the real world, no use of learning technology can adequately accomplish that goal because of the rapid pace at which hardware and software changes.

Solution: At-risk students struggle with managing environmental, social, and academic expectations. They often bring a multitude of issues to the classroom requiring teachers to find speedy and appropriate ways to help them to succeed in spite of their challenges. Technology is becoming more recognized as an alternate method of instruction for at-risk students. Also, students may find computers provide an accurate and unbiased response to their work; and both student–teacher relationships, and student–student interactions, change to one of help and collaboration.

Another bonus for using technology is to stimulate motivation and self-esteem. Through either personal experience or a review of the literature, many innovators perceived the dramatic effects that technology can have on students' interest in class activities and their sense of their own capabilities. Research supports that low-SES students benefit greatly from the use of technology because students feel a sense of equity within the classroom.

Finally, technology offers enriched learning environments and changes to the role of learners, two important elements for teaching at-risk learners. The use of technology contributes to the increased success rates for at-risk learners. For instance, students could work at their own pace, and return to the materials often. This was vital as when in traditional classrooms these learners struggled to keep up with the other students. Also, students could freely ask for help privately through email without the embarrassment of asking simple or repeated questions.

Technology Goals

- Classrooms serving at-risk students are collaborative. Students of varying abilities share information and work together in teams to make decisions and solve problems. Class activities are structured around student involvement in challenging, long-term projects and meaningful, engaged learning.
- All students have opportunities to use a variety of modern technologies—including a range of software applications, telecommunications, and video—to support their work on challenging, authentic tasks.
- Teachers have the knowledge and expertise to design and implement projects in which students work together on inquiry, design, and development supported by technology tools.
- School and district administrators, parents, and community members foster the provision of challenging, technology-supported learning opportunities within schools serving at-risk students.
- Administrators and teachers focus on the intersection of learning and technology, so that engaged learning and high technology performance contribute to the students' technology effectiveness.

- Schools and districts improve school facilities so that technology can be used in challenging ways with all students.
- Develop a strategy for giving all students adequate access to technology.
- Address policy issues in using technology for engaged learning.
- Ensure that school facilities are adequate for supporting technology networking that fosters engaged learning.
- Secure sources of on-site technical support to answer teacher and student questions and to keep the technology running smoothly.

TEACHERS FEEL INADEQUATELY PREPARED AND UNSUPPORTED AS THEY TRY TO EDUCATE STUDENTS WHO ARE AT RISK

Teachers with limited knowledge, passé practices, and low expectations are not appropriate candidates to work with at-risk students. Changing teacher expectations is a challenging undertaking, as expectations for student achievement often hinges on personal beliefs. Low expectations for student learning may result in less-challenging and ineffective instructional methods. If teachers embrace the idea that there is little they can do to improve at-risk student achievement, they find little incentive to change their instructional practices.

In addition, teachers must seize the opportunity to gain new knowledge and best practices designed to increase student engagement and improve performance. Today, the view of leadership is challenged to focus on scientific understandings of teaching and learning, data-driven decision making, and a broader view of professional development and PLCs so that all students can be successful. But it is crucial that school leaders provide appropriate professional development for teachers, in order for them to provide relevant learning experiences for at-risk students.

To ensure that learning is uninterrupted, the safety of students and protection of staff, school employees need to be trained on appropriate professional boundaries with students and how to exemplify the highest ethical standards. Adults working with the at-risk population should be devoted to their safety, well-being, and academic achievements. Yet, school staff may unexpectedly find themselves in a compromising situation with a student. This is often the result of poor choices and/or a lack of training regarding the dangers of certain behaviors by the school employee.

For example, a teacher builds a trusting relationship with a student, preventing the student from dropping out of school, and the student is about to graduate from high school. The teacher sees the student smoking marijuana on school grounds. If the teacher reports the incident, the school's discipline policy may result in the student being expelled. If the teacher withholds the information to protect the student, the teacher is ethically noncompliant. With professional ethics training and support, the teacher would be clear on his or her ethical and legal obligations.

Oftentimes, the inappropriate conduct is sexual in nature. Any school employee's misconduct or sexual abuse involving children destroys trust and negatively impacts an entire school community. What media coverage and notoriety of these situations has made clear is that schools and school employees need clear guidelines to follow regarding what to do when rumors of sexual abuse situations or suspicions arise.

Employee handbooks should include a code of conduct that clearly sets forth an employee's obligations and responsibilities toward students in: acting as role models of appropriate behavior; setting and maintaining appropriate boundaries with students; repercussions if an employee violates these obligations; how the school will respond; and the possible disciplinary consequences.

Overall, it is imperative that all independent school faculty and staff understand and appreciate their duty to provide a safe environment for students. Maintaining healthy relationships and boundaries with students is crucial to protecting students from harm. In addition, taking actions in response to situations that occur, such as an observation of a boundary crossing by another employee, or complying with mandatory reporting obligations, is also critical. For that reason, every employee should read and be familiar with the school's handbooks and policies.

The safety and well-being of students should be the highest priority of any school. Dealing with educator sexual misconduct involves a full program of risk management that every school must take seriously, including developing written guidelines setting forth expectations of behavior and reporting obligations; training employees about the school's policies, procedures, and expectations; educating students about where to go for help; responding quickly and appropriately to all allegations

The guidelines should cover both proactive steps that schools and employees should take to help prevent situations from occurring, as well as the appropriate and necessary responsive actions that the employees and school should take when situations arise. Schools must continue to re-address the guidelines to ensure that they are providing the safest environment possible.

Some reminders of what every school should do:

1. Clearly state and publicize the sexual harassment and abuse policy and complaint procedure. Every educational institution must have a policy that prohibits sexual harassment and sexual abuse. That policy must be repeatedly communicated to employees, students, parents, and the public. Here, once is clearly not enough. The policy must include a clear procedure for making complaints of sexual harassment or abuse

and prohibit any retaliation against persons who make a complaint or participate in an investigation.

2. Talk about the policy often, make it a part of orientation, and provide periodic reminders.

3. Teach students about what is prohibited. This includes a discussion of the meaning of "consent," how to make a complaint, and the consequences of violating the policy.

4. Empower students and parents to report violations. Make clear that no violation of the policy is permitted and that identifying and stopping violations are essential to achieving your school's mission. Remind staff of their fundamental responsibility to report suspected violations. Although groundless bad-faith allegations should not be permitted, employees should be encouraged to report good-faith suspicions and understand that eyewitness or irrefutable proof is not needed.

5. Train staff to identify sexual harassment and abuse, and the persons to whom such acts must be reported. Provide special training to persons designated to receive or investigate complaints.

6. Always advise complainants of their right to file criminal charges.

7. Thoroughly investigate and take appropriate action. If criminal charges are filed, the school still has an obligation to investigate and take any needed corrective action, though the process may be delayed for the short period of time the police needs to conduct its investigation. The criminal standard of guilt—beyond a reasonable doubt—does not apply. Rather, the standard is "the preponderance of evidence," or "more likely than not." If the policy has been violated, you must take action to protect the complainant and stop the behavior.

8. Do not promise the complainant confidentiality, and do not believe that your obligation to investigate and act can be determined by the desires of the complainant. In some cases, you may be required to disclose the identity of the complainant. You must investigate complaints to the best of the school's ability, and it must take appropriate action to address violations.

9. Reports are serious matters, but if you have a good-faith basis to believe a reportable offense has occurred, do not be frozen into inaction because you have some level of uncertainty. State your concern accurately.

10. Schools should promptly review their policies and practices both to ensure that these steps will be taken and to ensure that their policies and practice demonstrate the commitment to the principle that sexual harassment and abuse have no place at school.

Solution: At-risk students are experts at knowing how people tick; it is a survival skill. They know what to say and when to say it to get strategic reactions, create drama, or keep people away from them. They study their environment (often unknowingly) and are incredibly deliberate when they speak or act. It is because of their expertise that teachers need to be well aware of their own thoughts, feelings, and prejudices and seek support as needed.

ESSENTIAL IDEAS TO REMEMBER

Knowing student triggers will help you to develop an action plan for when they begin to escalate a situation. And if these troubled students can get you or the other students fuming, you will most likely forget about the fact that you are actually trying to teach them. If you find yourself becoming overly emotional about something a student did or said, take the time to determine the cause. Evaluate yourself on a consistent basis and work to remain objective, despite your innate feelings.

Build positive and structured relationships with your students. Notice that I say relationships, not friendships. Many unreachable students have not had positive interactions with adult authority figures, especially in a school environment. So, not only are you often having to break through negative stereotypes about teachers, you may also have to break through gender, cultural, generational, and socioeconomic stereotypes.

Building relationships is not about developing a friendship with a student, because liking you does not equate to respecting you or valuing what you have to say. Building relationships is about you making an effort to try to understand what the student is going through and laying a foundation for the student to eventually trust you. Relationships start with trust and consistency. Unfortunately, many of today's struggling youth have had little exposure to either of these concepts.

Present clear expectations from the beginning. One of the biggest complaints I hear from teachers is that their students are not performing to their standards, academically or behaviorally. My first question to these teachers is, "Do you have clear expectations of what you want, and have you effectively communicated those expectations to your students?" You may still run into students who refuse to meet expectations; however, more often than not, I find teachers with vague and ever-changing expectations.

If you are not clear about your standards, how can you expect your students to know what you want? Please do not assume your students should just know what to do and how to do it. If they did not need the skill, they would not need a teacher. Additionally, your standards need to be enforced fairly and consistently in order to be effective. Inconsistency and unequal treatment can and will be pointed out to you and possibly used against you.

Finally, separate the student from his or her choices and behavior. This advice is easier given than implemented. Misconduct is not an innate character flaw. Instead, it's simply an action that needs to be addressed, re-directed, or cleaned up. When a student misbehaves, the behavior must be addressed. When a teacher starts identifying a student as a problem, the teacher may lose objectivity and stop looking for the good the student is capable of achieving. We can love the child without loving his or her behavior choices. Here are tips that will support at-risk transformation:

A. Convey Expectations Clearly

Once at-risk students are identified, make sure that they know exactly what is expected of them. While more successful students might not need to hear this explicitly, it is very important that at-risk students be told what they are required to do to succeed. Consider which classroom rules are most important and post them on the wall. You might even have students sign a contract at the beginning of the term agreeing to these rules. Remember to convey these expectations in a friendly, nonconfrontational manner.

B. Give Choices to At-Risk Students

Some at-risk students become frustrated and act out at the lack of choice in the school environment. Do what you can to make at-risk students feel as though they have freedom of choice in the classroom. If a student is having a difficult time concentrating on an assignment, you might ask him whether he would like to keep going and try to finish it, or start a different assignment and pick this one back up at another time.

C. Use Real-Life Connections to Motivate

At-risk students sometimes have difficulty paying attention because they are uninterested in course material. Make lessons relevant to their lives by connecting them to real-life situations. While teaching math, try using football scores to teach arithmetic or algebra. While teaching a civics lesson, use an example from their world to illustrate it, and ask students their opinions. Be mindful, however, of the tendency for at-risk students to go off topic and turn your connections into inappropriate examples.

D. Reduce Anxiety by Reducing Competition

In some cases, at-risk students get stressed out by a competitive environment, and risk falling further behind. Try to eliminate competitiveness by fostering a communal atmosphere in the classroom. Avoid situations where students who volunteer the wrong answer out loud are too intimidated to speak again.

Instead, show students that wrong answers are always a necessary step for arriving at the right answer.

E. Adopt a Diverse Curriculum

Provide a variety of ways for students to communicate, learn, and complete work. This includes demonstrations, graphical explanations, extra resources, and self-assessments. Adding enriched curriculum will give students additional resources to learn. Be diligent about communications. Post announcements and updates frequently, respond quickly to email messages from students, and work directly with students by email and/or social networking. Help them to experience success by giving positive feedback that emphasizes what they do well. Allow these students the opportunity to choose what suits them best.

F. Develop Structure

At-risk students need structure in order to move through the curriculum. Providing possible organizers such as calendars, webpage postings, email announcements, digital work plans, or a list of deadlines proves to be helpful. Making these available for and accessible by the student gives clear expectations, and provides good leadership. Also, teachers should be flexible with due dates in order to encourage students to comply with the expectations for passing the course.

G. Establish a Safe Learning Environment

One of the most important aspects for teaching at-risk learners using technology is to provide a safe learning environment where everyone is accepted and supported. Ways to provide this include showing open acceptance to all students online or in class, communicating often with them, and encouraging versus reprimanding them for poor or late work. Developing a trusting relationship with these students is an important element, and one they may have never had with another teacher. Being patient with these students is vital.

Also, physical safety is typically at the top of most schools' lists for students, which is why there are metal detectors, drug dogs, and so on. However, emotional safety is often overlooked in classrooms. Emotional safety must be developed in order for students to learn. Do not allow students to make negative comments about each other. Most, if not all, school districts are addressing bullying issues, but there are things that should be done at the classroom level in order to make sure each student feels safe. Take a hard line on bullying and do not allow the psychological mind games to occur within the classroom.

H. Give Students a Way Out or the Ability to Have a Clean Slate

Many students are great at backing themselves into a corner. Unfortunately, they do not seem to have the same ability to get back out again. In many instances, an at-risk student would rather save face in front of his or her classmates than do what is right. Remember that your mission is to educate and maintain an environment conducive to learning. If a student is always in the "naughty corner," what motivation does he or she have to do well? Give students a way to make things right, to start fresh. Once he or she is labeled as the "troublemaker," you will only see a student who makes trouble. Do not hold a grudge.

I. Recognize That Negative Behaviors Are Serving a Purpose

If you only focus on and deal with "the behaviors," you are only treating the symptoms of the problem. Make an effort to get to the root of the issue. Perhaps if you can solve the issue, the symptoms will decrease or even disappear. For example, if a student continuously comes to school or class late, you could spend all of your time harping on the student and punishing him or her for being late, which does not change the undesired behavior. Or, you could try to figure out the reason in order to help the student be a better problem-solver. Do not assume to always know the reason for negative behaviors, either.

J. Believe in Your Students

Too many people look at students and make judgments based on their looks, their files, or their initial presentation of themselves. This judgment, over years and years, takes a toll on the students' self-esteem. Often, students do not believe in the best in themselves because they have been constantly reminded of how they are lacking. They will underplay their abilities in order to not fail to meet expectations. Every student has redeemable qualities; sometimes buried, but always there. Believing in unruly teens can be an act of faith, but you might be surprised at what you will find when you set out to look for the good things.

K. Allow Students to Feel Successful and Join in the Celebration

Self-esteem plays a major role in the choices of at-risk students. Many students who act out typically feel awful about themselves. Feeling miserable all of the time becomes cyclical; the student feels bad, makes bad choices, gets in trouble, feels bad for getting in trouble or for disappointing others, then makes more bad choices; and the saga continues. You may not be able to completely break students' cycles of poor self esteem, but you do have the ability to create a learning environment where students can feel successful. Let them tackle tough problems, have high expectations, and allow them to bask in their achievement, no matter how small.

Conclusion

Addressing school violence is the most significant hazard schools face today and should be *every* school district's priority. Cost-free strategies can be easily implemented and will significantly improve school safety while the more secure measures are being fully implemented. In addition, school leaders must implement programs and practices to help prevent at-risk students from dropping out of school and eliminate programs and practices that are contradictory to that mission.

We find that successful programs designed to educate at-risk students quickly identify at-risk characteristics and address them with fidelity. The students are then separated from other students and placed in classrooms that create a community atmosphere of compassion, accountability, responsibility, empowerment, and sincerity.

At-risk students will remain a part of school culture and society as a whole. Meeting the social-emotional needs of students at risk must come before academics. Fostering the belief that order comes before learning, the root causes of at-risk behaviors must be identified and addressed before learning can take place. Appropriate supports need to be in place to provide these students with the necessary tools needed to cope and transform.

The team working with at-risk students is highly trained and dedicated, communicating a concise vision, core values, and mission statements. They appropriately use a succinct comprehensive behavior system, invoking SAS as needed to assist students and their families in chronic or crisis situations. The team closely monitors the progress of students through an ISP. They collaborate regularly to ensure that all student needs are identified and addressed.

School can be tough on many students, but it is especially difficult for at-risk students to focus on academic and school expectations when they are barely surviving in other parts of their lives. Academic success may be important to them, but they frequently lack the skills to perform well and require additional support, which they often reject. Students' confidence rises when they are able to accomplish what is expected of them. Academic success equals hope for the future, something many at-risk students desperately seek.

The education and evolution of at-risk students is an enormous task that requires tenacity and commitment from students, parents, and schools.

Students should:

- Accept responsibility for choices made
- Accept support
- Participate in the rehabilitation process whole-heartedly
- Understand that change doesn't occur overnight

Parents should:

- Recognize the need for help
- Seek support
- Utilize alternative placement options for rehabilitation purposes
- Be consistent and supportive

Schools should:

- Create schools-within-schools and interdisciplinary teams of teachers and support staff to encourage a sense of belonging
- Hold students to high educational standards and communicate the belief that all students can succeed
- Foster resiliency by building on students' strengths rather than focusing on "deficits"
- Implement a succinct behavior system
- Involve family, community, and other support services in educating and supporting students' social and academic needs
- Offer families alternative placements for rehabilitation purposes *only*

Student needs, interests, and abilities are the teachers' focus as they prepare the learning environment by using best practices that encourage students to deepen their understanding of content. Data-driven decisions provide maximum support to educators who administer RtI. The curriculum chosen boasts multiple learning strategies that address the various learning styles and, whenever possible, are related to real-world careers.

Finally, implementing a comprehensive, integrated behavior system requires policies that facilitate blending many resources. This includes possibly restructuring to combine parallel efforts supported by various funding sources. By fully implementing effective programs and concise policies, the school-home-community operates synergistically. The end product is a cohesive and powerful school–home–community partnership, equipped to educate and transform the lives of at-risk students throughout the nation.

Glossary

3-prong map	The tool designed to address the progression of at-risk student behavior.
Adversities	Challenges due to underemployment, poor health, lack of resources, personal trials, and so on. *Remedy*: Implement wraparound services to provide a link between family adversity and the at-risk student and family.
At-risk student	A student who is in danger of academic failure is often labeled "at risk."
At-risk youth	Youth are considered at risk when they experience a significant mismatch between their circumstances and needs.
Court involvement	At-risk behaviors generally lead to court involvement. *Remedy*: Develop ongoing partnerships with agencies who maintain age-appropriate and comprehensive programs that require adult advocates and family participation.
Experiencing limited success in school	Students experiencing limited success in school are often unable to choose the right subjects, attend classes regularly, listen and take good notes, study daily, and get involved in school activities. *Remedy*: Schools educating at-risk students must hire the most dedicated and caring staff in order to replenish the lack of students feeling successful in school.
Impulsivity	Students who act impulsively do not consider the consequences of their behavior before they act. *Remedy*: Keep communication lines open and discuss the student's behaviors and feelings, not the adult's.
Individual service plan (ISP)	A form designed to identify the characteristic(s) causing a student to be at risk, and monitoring his/her progress during the intervention process.
Low academic achievers	Typically, at-risk students earn lower-than-average grades. *Remedy*: Schools educating at-risk students must hire teachers with substantive content knowledge and above-average pedagogical skills to meet students' academic and/or behavior needs.
Low socioeconomic status (SES)	Families from low-socioeconomic-status communities are less likely to have the financial resources available to provide children with academic support. *Remedy*: Invoke collaborative resources that directly improve the quality of students' lives living in low-SES communities.

Mental health disorders	Mental health disorders such as attention deficit hyperactivity disorder may interfere with a student's ability to function at school. *Remedy*: If unable to defuse the crisis, quickly seek professional help.
School-within-a-school	A smaller educational unit with a separate educational program, its own staff and students, and its own budget.
Student advocacy support (SAS)	A systematic intervention for students demonstrating at-risk behaviors.
Truancy	Students who are regularly absent or tardy to school. *Remedy*: Adopt policies that support a comprehensive truancy-reduction program to achieve positive outcomes.
Uninterested in school activities	Unproductive students are not committed to participating in school activities. *Remedy*: Provide students with a deeper understanding of content to enhance their appreciation for learning, which leads to an appreciation for school.
Victimization	In many cases, at-risk students have been the victim of violence by adults, relatives, or other children in their lives. *Remedy*: Provide disciplinary consequences from counseling to alternate placement for noncompliance of the bullying policy. Envokes SAS for other reports of abuse.

References

Boykin, A. Wade and Pedro Noguera. *Creating the Opportunity to Learn: Moving from Research to Practice to Close the Achievement Gap, 1st edition*. Alexandria, VA: Association for Supervision & Curriculum Development, 2011.

Bridgeland, John M., John J. DiIulio Jr., and Karen Burke Morison. "The Silent Epidemic: Perspectives of High School Dropouts," *Civic Enterprises*. Bill & Melinda Gates foundation, n.d.

DuFour, Richard, Robert Eaker, and Rebecca DuFour. *Revisiting Professional Learning Communities at Work: New Insights for Improving Schools*. Bloomington, IN: Solution Tree, 2008.

Eisley, Loren. "The Star Thrower," in *The Unexpected Universe*. San Diego: Harcourt, Brace and World, 1969.

Lipsey, Mark W., and James H. Derzon. "Predictors of Violent and Serious Delinquency in Adolescence and Early Adulthood: A Synthesis of Longitudinal Research." In Rolf Loeber and David P. Farrington, eds., *Serious and Violent Juvenile Offenders: Risk Factors and Successful Interventions*. Thousand Oaks, CA: Sage Publications, 1998.

Loeber, Rolf, and Farrington, David P. *Serious and Violent Juvenile Offenders: Risk Factors and Successful Interventions*. Thousand Oaks, CA: Sage Publications, 1998.

Milner, H. Richard. *Start Where You Are, But Don't Stay There: Understanding Diversity, Opportunity Gaps, and Teaching in Today's Classrooms*. Cambridge, MA: Harvard Education Press, 2010.

Noguera, Pedro A. *The Trouble With Black Boys: And Other Reflections on Race, Equity, and the Future of Public Education, 1st edition*. San Francisco: Jossey-Bass, 2009.

Noguera, Pedro and Edward Fergus. *Invisible No More: Understanding the Disenfranchisement of Latino Men and Boys*. New York: Routledge, 2011.

Peters, Stephen G. *Teaching to Capture and Inspire All Learners: Bringing Your Best Stuff Every Day!* Thousand Oakes, CA: Corwin Press, 2007.

Taylor-Gibson, Joyce. *Educating the Throw-away Children: What We Can Do to Help Students at Risk*. Hoboken, NJ: Jossey-Bass, 1997.

Wiggins, Grant, and Jay McTighe. *Understanding by Design, 1st ed.* Alexandria, VA: Association for Supervision & Curriculum Development, 2011.

About the Author

Charisse Beach is an educator and subject-matter expert on transforming and educating at-risk students in grades 6–12. Beach is former principal of Premier Academy, a Regional Safe School Program serving grades 6–12 from Grundy, Kendall, and Will Counties in Illinois. Currently, she is an assistant principal in Joliet Illinois School District 86 and an Illinois State Board of Education presenter who conducts professional-development training for school administrators on transforming and educating students demonstrating at-risk behaviors.

Beach developed and implemented a three-prong behavior map that resulted in a 79 percent reduction in out-of-school suspensions as well as implemented a Student Advocacy Support (SAS) system for students in need of additional wraparound support services. Under her leadership, an average of 83 percent of students transitioned back to their home schools at or above grade level with sufficient credits to graduate.

Beach holds a bachelor of arts degree in English with a secondary education teaching certificate and a minor in psychology and a master of arts degree in educational administration. She maintains national memberships in Court Appointed Special Advocates (CASA) and the American Society for Training and Development (ASTD). She is the founder of At-Risk Students: Education & Evolution, a training and development program designed to educate, train, and equip educators with practical strategies on how to transform at-risk youth. She is also the cofounder of Youth Transformation Services, an organization that helps at-risk youth achieve academic, personal, and social success.

Beach currently resides in Joliet, Illinois and is the mother of two sons, Robert and Oliver, and one grandson, Elijah.